Historic Restaurants
OF
CINCINNATI

Historic Restaurants

OF

CINCINNATI

THE QUEEN CITY'S TASTY HISTORY

DANN WOELLERT

AMERICAN PALATE

Published by American Palate
A Division of The History Press
Charleston, SC 29403
www.historypress.net

Front cover images, from left to right, top to bottom: Habig's Restaurant sign, West Pharmacy Soda Fountain, Frisch's Drive-In and Caproni's Restaurant.

First published 2015

Manufactured in the United States

ISBN 978.1.46711.764.7

Library of Congress Control Number: 2015943186

To my mother, Flora, whose wonderful home cooking inspired me to become the foodie that I am.

CONTENTS

PREFACE

C incinnati is one of those weird food cities. Our mishmash of immigrant groups has invented food dishes and consumer food brands that can be found nowhere else in the country. Foods like our chili, goetta and mock turtle soup were invented here and stay here. Skyline Chili found that out when it tried to expand its franchising out of the Tristate area without success. We elevate these foods to pop status and celebrate them at family restaurants, churches and commercial food festivals throughout the year. Are we in Cincinnati a city more receptive to new food ideas than other areas of the country? Or are we just frugal and flexible? Sure, we've been victims of mega food trends throughout the decades like smorgasbords and fondue. But we also seem to have a level of food genius that lets our culinary minds create new and innovative foods.

There are many restaurants that have come and gone in Greater Cincinnati over the years, and there's no way to touch on every single one of them in one book. I've tried to pay homage to those classic Cincinnati restaurants that have been around the longest, have reached landmark status or had a major impact on dining culture in Cincinnati.

We have many restaurants in Cincinnati that have been around more than fifty years and are going strong. We even have four still-operating restaurants that are more than one hundred years old! A few of our classics are even reportedly haunted. The recession and new food trends have recently put several classics out of business, however. So enjoy and reminisce about your

Cincinnati food experiences as I take you back to and through some of Cincinnati's classic restaurants.

I'd like to thank the following for their help: Pat Gramglia of the Pasquale Pizza family; Pete Buscani, executive vice-president of LaRosa's; John Frank of Frank Tea & Spice Company; Billy Lambrinides of the Skyline Chili family; the Daoud family of Gold Star and Charlie Howard, VP of marketing for Gold Star; Dan Glier of Glier's Goetta; Gaynell Sizemore of Empire Chili; Bill Kahn of the Chili Bowl; Karen Haggis of the Haggis and Manoff chili families; the wonderful folks at the history and genealogy department of the Main Cincinnati Public Library; Valda Moore at Price Hill Historical Society; the University of Cincinnati Library; my commissioning editor, Krista Slavicek; and my parents, Roger and Flora.

Chapter 1
EARLY CINCINNATI FOOD

Cincinnati is a receptive and fertile ground for creating new food categories that exist nowhere else in the world. While the city's patina is most certainly Germanic, there are a number of other ethnicities that have made their marks on its culinary history. The Macedonians influenced what is arguably the most popular regional item: Cincinnati-style chili. The Jewish faithful have had immense influence on the local food. The heavy Catholic influence in the area has made Lenten fish dishes popular year-round. And the few Italian communities have made their marks and given us their perspectives on comfort food.

There are food wars still raging that split households—brother against mother, father against daughter. When it comes to the chili trenches, you are either with Skyline or Gold Star—or your local neighborhood chili parlor. On the ice cream front, you are either on the side of Graeter's or Aglamesis. And you either eat your goetta crispy or non-crispy. Finally, the pumpkin pie wars are split almost equally between Buskens and Frisch's.

Food is also heavily influenced by the Eastside/Westside divide. The Westside of Cincinnati can be loosely defined as the area west of Interstate 75 and the area south of the Western Hills Viaduct to the western city limits. This area is very German Catholic, and many families stay within the neighborhoods of their original parishes for three or more generations. The Eastside is loosely defined as the area south of the Norwood Lateral and east of Interstate 71 to the eastern city limits. Eastsiders are more transient than Westsiders. Until only a few years ago, you could not find a Thai restaurant in

Cincinnati's Westside, and until recently, dishes like hanky panky, goetta and fish logs could not be found in the Eastside. Now even the hipster Rookwood Pottery in Mount Adams on the Eastside serves goetta hanky panky, a fusion of two traditionally Westside Germanic dishes.

Cincinnati's first tavern and eatery, the Square and Compass Tavern Inn, was owned and operated by an early pioneer named Griffin Yeatman, who had arrived in 1793. It overlooked the public landing, which would later be named Yeatman's Cove after him. The name of the tavern is a reference to the symbol of the Masonic order to which he belonged. The tavern became a hub for the community, being the site of the post office, the site of the first territorial legislature and Supreme Court and the site of many Masonic

Thefe are to fignify to all Perfons that I have opened a Tavern of Public Entertainment at the Cove, having recently come from Virginia. All fhall be well entertained at a reafonable rate.

GRIFFIN YEATMAN

Griffin Yeatman, Cincinnati's first tavern owner, and the ad he placed to promote his opening. *Courtesy of the Public Library of Cincinnati and Hamilton County.*

banquets. His establishment was patronized by the likes of the Marquis de Lafayette, Andrew Jackson, Aaron Burr, William Henry Harrison, "Mad" Anthony Wayne and George Rogers Clark.

As the city began to grow out of a fort and early pioneer settlement, early taverns like the Blue Goose and the Hotel of the Golden Lamb in Cumminsville were feeding the hungry Irish and German canal workers in the 1820s. You might see a passenger pigeon potpie or stuffed gamehen, froglegs or turtle soup on the menu. By 1819, there were seventeen taverns in Cincinnati, with accommodations being hard to secure with the high volumes of travelers coming to the Queen City. In 1817, John Palmer, a traveler to Cincinnati, wrote about the tavern food, "Five dollars per week is the price of the best hotel in Cincinnati. We paid $3 per week, had a room to ourselves and our living was excellent: at breakfast plenty of beef steak, bacon and eggs, white bread, Johnny cakes [of cornmeal], butter, tea and coffee. Dinner—two or three dishes of fowl, roast meats, kidney beans, peas, new potatoes, preserves, cherry pie, etc. Supper—nearly the same as breakfast."

In 1832, an English woman named Frances Trollope published *Domestic Manners of Americans*, based on her travels through America and her three-year residence in Cincinnati, still a frontier town. She was not very fond of Cincinnati, its wine or food and its people, earning her the name "Old Madam Vinegar." She was appalled at the hordes of pigs she encountered on the streets being led to the slaughterhouses, as well as the number of pig parts and blood discarded by them. Trollope pointed out with disgust how Cincinnatians devoured watermelons in public, spitting seeds and their chins dripping with juices like Neanderthals.

The wealthy of Cincinnati were eating very well at this time. An excerpt from the diary of a wealthy Englishwoman, Isabella Trotter—who, with her husband, was entertained by the Longworth family—gives us an idea of the lavishness of Cincinnati hospitality:

Wednesday the 27th [of November 1858] *Mrs.* [Catherine] *Anderson, Mr. Longworth's daughter called and asked us to spend that evening also at her mother's house…*

We had quails and Cincinnati hams, also oysters served in three different ways—stewed, fried in butter, and in their natural state, but taken out of their shells and served en masse in a large dish. Our friends were astonished that we did not like these famous oysters of theirs in any form, which we did not, they being very huge in size, and strong in flavor. We said, too, we did not like making the two bites of any oyster, they pitied our want of taste, and lamented over our miserably small ones in England.

Toward ten o'clock a table was laid out in the drawing room with their Catawba champagne, which was handed round in tumblers, followed by piles of vanilla ice a foot and a half high. There were two of these towers of Babel, on the table, and each person was given a supply that would have served for half a dozen in England; the cream however, is so light in this country that a great deal more can be taken of it than in England; ices are extremely good and cheap all over America; even in small towns they are to be had as good as in the large ones. Water ices or fruit ices are rare, they are almost always of vanilla cream. In summer a stewed peach is sometimes added.

Probably no part of history has had its mark on our cuisine more than our relationship with our pork packing industry. No other industry had more impact on the city's economy, growth and culture than the processing of pigs and their porky byproducts. By 1850, pork production had reached a peak of more than 400,000 hogs, with forty-two processing plants. Cincinnati had become the world's largest dresser of pork. By the Civil War, more than 500,000 hogs would trot into Cincinnati's stockyards. It's no wonder that our city's mascot is the Flying Pig and our nickname "Porkopolis."

Originally, pork spare ribs were considered a throwaway part after slaughter. When the German immigrants in Cincinnati noticed that they were being thrown into the river by pork processors, they quickly realized that a cheap meat source could be had. One Philadelphian boarding in Cincinnati in the 1840s said of his landlady, "What a splendid table my landlady, Mrs. G___ keeps. She gives us spare ribs for breakfast four or five times a week, and the finest I ever tasted in my life." His friend, a native, said, "If your landlady knew you were so fond of them, I suppose she could give them to you every morning of your life. You don't appear to know that they cost her nothing. The fact is, she can get a basket filled at any pork house in the city by sending for them and not pay a cent."

Because transportation options were limited and expensive for farmers, they drove their pigs to market in Cincinnati on foot on the early turnpikes, like the Mount Pleasant and Hamilton Turnpike (or Hamilton Avenue) and the Colerain, Oxford, and Brookville Turnpike (or Colerain Avenue). Colerain Avenue became the road on which most of the livestock was driven to the Cincinnati stockyards. The drive was a slow process that required hotels and inns with pens for the farmers to stop overnight, eat and rest.

A lithograph that shows one of the many pork-processing plants in "Porkopolis." *Courtesy of the Public Library of Cincinnati and Hamilton County.*

There were such farmers' hotels on Colerain Avenue in Dunlap, Bevis, Groesbeck and Mount Airy. The Six Mile House on Colerain Avenue in Mount Airy was exactly six miles from the end of the turnpike in Brighton and was shown in the 1860s on local maps. It remained standing until the 1980s as a Westside landmark restaurant serving German-inspired and home-style food, liquor and entertainment. The Glen Airy House, also in Mount Airy, was noted in the *Venice Graphic* in 1887 as "possess[ing] all the requisites of a summer resort so far as beautiful scenery and excellent

A common nineteenth-century Cincinnati sight: hogs being driven to the slaughterhouse. *Courtesy of the Public Library of Cincinnati and Hamilton County.*

culinary service is concerned...all farmers who have occasion to travel to and fro along this Pike are sure to stop at the Glen Airy for refreshments of all kinds."

In Groesbeck, at the cross section of Colerain and Galbraith Road, were two farmers' hotels, Luichingers and Weisenhans, on the northern corners. The southern corners held livestock pens. The west side of Colerain Avenue and Dry Ridge Road housed the Bevis Tavern, built in 1855 by Jesse Bevis.

The last of these farmers' hotels still standing was built by Christopher Keller in 1859 on Colerain and Hoffner Street in Cumminsville across from the Wesleyan Cemetery. The first floor was the tavern and eatery, the second floor the boarding rooms and the third floor a ballroom. Outside, an irregular lot next to the hotel housed the pigpens for farmers' livestock.

After the Civil War, Chicago would take over as the "Hog Butcher to the World." Cincinnati continued to butcher more and more hogs with the opening of Union Stockyards in 1871 and completion of the Cincinnati Southern Railway in 1880, but it never would regain its title of global pork-processing capital. After World War I, driving livestock by foot was a thing of the past, and the hotels, taverns and roadhouses of the era were converted to other uses. The Union Stockyards closed in 1980, and the Kahn's plant on Spring Grove Avenue closed in 2006.

The last farmers' hotel standing, built in 1859 by Christopher Keller on Colerain Avenue in Cumminsville. *Courtesy of the author.*

The prevalence of cheap and readily available meat in Cincinnati gave birth to the many German sausages in our meat markets, as well as other pork-related dishes like city chicken and goetta. City chicken is a dish made up of cubes of pork that are skewered, battered and panfried. At the time in Cincinnati, pork was cheaper than chicken, and the skewered pork resembled a chicken leg.

As we became more and more industrialized, we looked to New York City for inspiration for our high-end cuisine. The St. Nicholas Hotel Restaurant at the corner of Fourth and Race was compared to Delmonico's in New York, which featured iconic American dishes like Lobster Newberry, Eggs Benedict, Chicken a la King, Manhattan Clam Chowder and even Baked Alaska.

The St. Nicholas was opened in 1865 by Balthazar Roth and was known worldwide for its cuisine, hospitality and social affairs; this did much to advertise Cincinnati as a world-class city. In addition to the main restaurant, the St. Nicholas also later housed the Auf Wiedersehen Tap Room, the Kneipe and a coffee shop.

Before the Civil War, single men in Cincinnati lived at boardinghouses, which included their daily fare of breakfast and dinner. By 1850, there were nearly two hundred boardinghouses in downtown Cincinnati. Those who

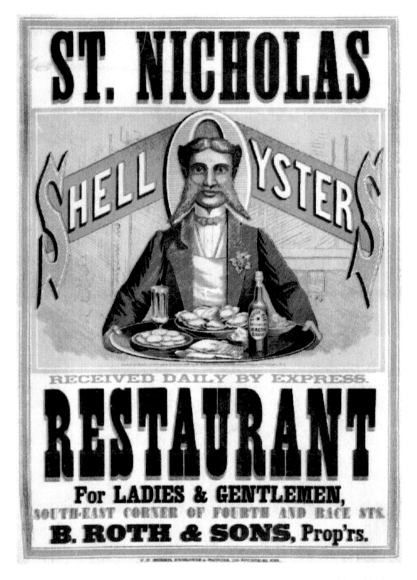

Poster advertising oysters at the St. Nicholas Hotel, which was opened in 1865 by Balthazar Roth. *Courtesy of the Public Library of Cincinnati and Hamilton County.*

could afford it would supplement their daily fare with sweets, oysters and bottled beverages at the variety of saloons, bars and coffeehouses in downtown as they networked with other enterprising young men and women.

The diary of Joseph Mersman, a German immigrant, gives a great picture of the eating life of a single middle-class German immigrant in the

BANK EXCHANGE HOTEL,

And Dining Rooms,

GEORGE SELVES, PROPRIETOR,

Third street, opposite the Franklin and

Lafayette Banks,

CINCINNATI.

An 1846 ad for the Bank Exchange Hotel shows turtles lining up to get decapitated to become turtle soup. *Courtesy of the Public Library of Cincinnati and Hamilton County.*

Over-the-Rhine neighborhood between 1848 and 1849. He and his circle of friends frequented German-owned places like Carl Rebstock's Coffeehouse at Fifteenth and Vine, where the nation's first Turnverein was founded. Other hangouts included the Bank Exchange Hotel restaurant at Third Street, famous for its turtle soup; William Tell's Coffeehouse at Fifth Street between Main and Walnut; the Black Bear Tavern at Sycamore and Ninth; Wellman's Coffeehouse at Main Street; and Mulholland's Coffeehouse at Sycamore and Eighth Streets. In the mid-nineteenth century, a coffeehouse was a place to drink beer, wine and spirits and get a small bite to eat.

Around the time of the Civil War, pigs' feet were the "buffalo wings" of Cincinnati—a cheap and popular bar snack on most menus around town. They were cheaper and more plentiful than oysters and so were nicknamed "Cincinnati oysters." Cincinnatians would also look forward to the spring and a local favorite: currant pie. In winter, they could also look forward to eggnog, which at the time meant eggs, cream and spices mixed with warm beer, cider, wine or spirits.

Oysters in America were viewed as very healthy and as aphrodisiacs in the ninetenth century. Cincinnati followed the trend of other U.S. cities and had oyster houses, oyster saloons and oyster bars before the Chesapeake Bay oyster beds began to deplete in the 1880s. Those beds, which produced 111 million pounds of oysters in the 1880s, now only produce about 3 million pounds annually. So many oysters were transported on ice from 1835 to 1850 between the Atlantic coast and Cincinnati that the stagecoach line was called the Oyster Line. This oyster-bearing trip by stagecoach was a five-day affair. Oysters were to nineteenth-century Cincinnatians what Chinese food became for their twentieth-century descendants.

One of the most famous of the Cincinnati oyster houses, the Central Oyster House at 120 East Fourth Street, had been in business since 1893 and served Cincinnatians their beloved aphrodisiacs into the 1970s. Jake Rosenfeld opened the restaurant in 1893 near Washington Park, specializing in oyster dishes. His nephew, Jake Spencer, kept the traditional recipes until he closed the restaurant in 1974.

An 1858 menu from Cincinnati's Gibson House showed that it served oysters in just about any way you could imagine: baked in shells, escalloped, baked with finer herbs, in small oyster pies, raw, baked in a form, stewed with champagne, baked with cheese, fried, pickled, in a cold salad and even in aspic.

Around the time of the Civil War, wild game was still very common, even in the high-class hotel and restaurant settings. Dishes that today seem a bit too gamey for our tastes were served at Cincinnati hotels around the holidays. Some of these dishes included Bear Ribs with Pouvorada Sauce (a peppery French sauce); Broiled Squirrels with Stewart Sauce; Virginia Opossum, Kentucky Style; Stuffed Tennessee Coon with Plain Gravy; and Rabbits Larded with Champagne Sauce.

From the 1870s into the 1890s, the wealthy of Cincinnati got a taste of President Thomas Jefferson's kitchen. Peter Fossett, a popular Cincinnati caterer to the wealthy of Cincinnati, was born in 1815 into slavery at Thomas Jefferson's Monticello. His mother, Edith, was Jefferson's favorite cook, and

A menu cover from Cincinnati's longest-running oyster house. *Courtesy of the Public Library of Cincinnati and Hamilton County.*

Left: A portrait of Reverend Peter Fossett, whose catering uplifted Cincinnati cuisine in the late nineteenth century. *Courtesy of Monticello National Historic Site.*

Below: At Bellevue House atop the Bellevue Incline, guests expected a lively time. *Courtesy of the Public Library of Cincinnati and Hamilton County.*

his father, Joseph, was the slave foreman of carpentry. Peter's first cousin was Sally Hemings, the famous consort who bore five of Jefferson's slave children. Sally accompanied Jefferson to Paris when he was ambassador to France, and there he learned the fine art of French cooking, taking it back to the Monticello kitchen staff. Fossett became knowledgeable in French cooking and knew how to prepare for high-end events. Growing up among household servants, he helped his mother and the other house servants cater to visitors like Presidents James Madison and John Adams and General Lafayette. The Fossetts catered benefits, balls and private parties to the wealthy industry barons of Cincinnati in their homes and at the high-end hotels around town.

In the 1870s, Cincinnati developed a unique form of dining in the hilltop resorts at the top of the inclines. Real estate developers wanted to draw people to the hills but needed to offer them a convenient way to get to the top. Each of the inclines had at its peak a fabulous resort drawing people out for a day of fresh air, celebration and sweeping views of the Ohio River Valley. Each incline house competed against the others for the best entertainment to draw visitors. As most of the entertainment was free, the houses depended on alcohol sales to support themselves. The most festive of all days at the hilltop resorts was Sunday. After 1882, when strict enforcement of Sunday closing laws in Cincinnati was enacted by the mayor, the resorts' business declined; most were defunct by the 1890s.

The Highland House was built atop the Mount Adams Incline in 1880. It could accommodate eight thousand people every day and included famed restaurants, beer gardens, a bowling alley, dance halls and a picnic grove. Considered the most highbrow of all the hilltop resorts, manager Frank Harff imported premier bands from around the world, and as a result, Cincinnati became known as the "Paris of America." Families, couples and singles alike put on their finery and celebrated the day. From any view at the Highland House, a visitor could count on enjoying a cold Moerlein beer, a great meal and wonderful surroundings. The Highland House closed in 1890 and was razed in 1895.

Chapter 2
THE GERMANIC INFLUENCE

The Germanic influence has left its mark deeper than any other ethnic group on Cincinnati culinary traditions. The influence has been diluted into a pan-German cuisine, as if people from all regions of what is now Germany ate the same food when they arrived in Cincinnati. This pan-German cuisine can be seen more regularly at church and city festivals and less so in specifically German restaurants around town. You will find more Germanic foods in family restaurants on the Westside of Cincinnati than you will on the Eastside. Cincinnati brats, sauerbraten, sauerkraut balls, goetta, hot slaw, mock turtle soup or schnitzel are items you will find on the menus at today's Germanic restaurants. In Cincinnati, any restaurant that carries the name "Garden" ensures an outdoor beer garden where German *gemutlickkeit* can be experienced. Although German and Austrian foods are probably the least trendy food category in the nation, Cincinnati has had a long history of German-themed restaurants, some lasting more than half a century.

The height of the German *bierstube*, or beer pub, was in the late nineteenth century and was concentrated in Over-the-Rhine. One of the most well known was Wielert's Pavilion, established in 1873 by Heinrich Wielert on Vine Street. Wielert was a Hanoverian immigrant, a member of the Cincinnati Central Turners and a Civil War veteran. Wielert's became the off-campus city hall during the reign of Republican boss George Cox, who arrived nightly at 5:00 p.m. to conspire with his cronies at his permanently reserved table. When political meetings happened at the Central Turnhall behind Wielert's on Walnut Street, Cox would send young boys as runners

A sketch by Henry Farney showing the activity at Wielert's saloon in its heyday. *Courtesy of the Public Library of Cincinnati and Hamilton County.*

to give him updates on what was going on. Gary Hermann, manager of the Cincinnati Reds, and Rudolph Hynicka, chairman of the Hamilton County Republican Party, were regular members of Cox's 5:00 p.m. table.

Wielert's was a high-class family resort where women and children would come with their families to be entertained. While orchestras played German music, vendors would walk around selling frankfurters and pretzels, and waiters would carry liter steins ten or more per hand to satisfy the thirsty Germanic patrons. If you didn't look at the menu, waiters would bring out the standard order of wienerschnitzel, German fried potatoes and rye bread with your beer. The beer garden spanned a block and was roofed but open on the sides. Busts of famous German musicians lined the walls.

Between Wielert's and the canal (now Central Parkway), there were at least seventeen other beer halls, among them Hildebrand's, Schickling's and Kissell's. Although it was closed permanently during Prohibition, Wielert's still stands today, largely intact, at 1410 Vine, a monument to our German beer hall heritage.

Because of laws preventing drinking on Sundays, Cincinnati's Germans could take a canalboat or the Cincinnati, Hamilton and Dayton Railroad outside the city limits on Sundays to Cumminsville, St. Bernard or Avondale to drink their beers and enjoy themselves. Cumminsville had Reichraths' Saloon, Poplar Grove and many other German beer gardens that catered to these special Sunday visitors. The problem with being outside of Cincinnati police jurisdiction was that they were not there when beer-related brawls happened, and the *Enquirer* reported many rough rumbles happening at these resorts.

Within the Over-the-Rhine and, later, West End German neighborhoods of Cincinnati, butchers had to cater to immigrants from all of the duchies, kingdoms and city states of Germany, which wasn't a unified country until 1871. Since every region had its own specialties, butchers would carry Bremen sausages for those from the northern region, currywurst for those from Lower Saxony and other specialties for immigrants from other areas of Germany. As these immigrants lived together closely and began to become familiar with one another's specialties, they fused and evolved into our city's two most common sausages: the Cincinnati mett, a red and often spicy sausage, both cured and smoked, and the Cincinnati brat, a white ground pork sausage with milk powder and herby spices. The closest sausage to our Cincinnati brat is probably the Bavarian weisswurst. The only difference is that our brat is encased in a normal casing and grilled, whereas the

Nasty Corner on Vine Street, where bars offered a wienerwurst with every drink. *Courtesy of the Public Library of Cincinnati and Hamilton County.*

weisswurst is made in a very thin casing and is blanched in water below the boiling point.

We in Cincinnati view sauerkraut on a brat as a condiment, while if you spooned it on a sausage or currywurst in northern Germany, they'd look at you like you had two heads. In Germany, sauerkraut is never a condiment—it's more of a side salad and usually only eaten by older folks for digestive purposes. Our American eat-while-you-walk convenience mentality is what turned sauerkraut from a side salad into a condiment.

Another Cincinnati German dish that's not a native to Germany is the sauerkraut ball. Mostly seen at German festivals in the summer, many restaurants serve them as appetizers. Some are simply deep-fried sauerkraut, while others have bits of pork sausage and cream cheese. They all come with a variety of dipping sauces. Although we believe that Cincinnati created the sauerkraut ball, Akron, Ohio, has a commercial producer, the OrDerv company, founded in 1964, so there is a rivalry in terms of whose came first. Cincinnati may not have a commercial producer, but every year our German festivals serve these balls every weekend from mid-August to the end of October. Our near neighbor, Waynesville, Ohio, has hosted its Sauerkraut Festival, with sauerkraut balls, since 1970. Restaurants like Mecklenburg Gardens in Clifton, Wunderbar and Hofbrauhaus in Newport, Lazslo's Iron Skillet in Newtown and Rascal's New York Deli in Blue Ash serve the balls, as did the Black Forest and Lenhardt's back in the day.

BRING IN THE SINGING BAKERS

Grammer's was founded in 1872 on Vine Street by a German immigrant baker named Anton Grammer. He built a café across from his bakery, which became the headquarters of the Cincinnati Baeckers Gesangverein, or German Baker's Singing Society. Anton's bakery and café clients were primarily other immigrant bakers whom he helped get on their feet in their new homeland. When Anton retired, he passed along the café to his bachelor son, Frank Grammer, who lived over the restaurant until he died in 1950. Frank built the present Grammer's on Walnut Street in 1911, on property of a Lutheran church he had demolished. He had a burled mahogany bar built by the Brunswick Company and the leaded glass entrance window that exists today built in Germany. It originally had a separate side entrance for the ladies for propriety.

Grammer's restaurant with its now removed neon sign. *Courtesy of Don Prout, Cincinnati Views.*

In the early 1900s, Grammer's thrived in Over-the-Rhine. The first room, with a 1920s panoramic mural of the Rhine River Valley, was the restaurant; the middle room was a billiards hall; and the back room was for regular customers. Like Wielert's political stammtisch, Grammer's was the regular stop for Mayor Russell Wilson in the 1930s, making many of the city's important decisions from his regular table.

The next owner, Charles Berkman, acquired the property in 1950 and ran the restaurant until 1962. Berkman turned Grammer's into a full-scale German eatery. It was then sold to a Hungarian, Karl Mohaupt Sr., who had boxed under the name Kid Mohawk. He continued the tradition of its German fare with menu items like wienerschnitzel and Tyroler apple strudel, a favorite. Former city councilman Jim Tarbell bought Grammer's from the Mohaupt family in 1984.

It was revived for a while in 2010 as a hipster dance club that hosted a yearly David Bowie Birthday Party, but it only lasted a few years and has been opened on special occasion for Midpoint Music Fest and Bockfest. Current owner Dan Wade wants to build condos around the original building, keeping the original Walnut Street façade and barroom.

Arnold's

Arnold's Bar and Grill is the oldest continually operating bar café in Cincinnati. The two buildings that make up Arnold's were built in the late 1840s. The bar side at 210 East Eighth Street was originally a barbershop, and the other side at 208 East Eighth Street was a feed store, with the adjoining courtyard used as a livery. It was founded in 1861 by Samuel Arnold, a billiard table maker who bought half of a three-story property. He put his family on the third floor, rented rooms on the second and operated a simple tavern on the first.

Samuel's son, Hugo, took over in the late 1890s and bought out the tannery and feed store portion of the building. The new ground-floor room on the other side served as a ladies' waiting room, as women weren't served in the bar and even had their own entrance.

A third generation took over in the 1920s when Hugo's son, Elmer, stepped up with some reluctance. He was accustomed to the life on the road as a horseshoe nail salesman, but he came to like being a tavern owner, even during Prohibition. Elmer added a kitchen and turned Arnold's into a café, but he didn't stop selling liquor. It was during Elmer's ownership that odd buzzers and hiding places in walls and floors were built that later owners discovered. These could only have been used during Prohibition to alert and hide the hooch when officers came for inspection.

The Arnold family sold in 1959 to Greek brothers Jim Christakos and George Christakos. Jim was a former professional wrestler nicknamed the "Greek God" and was rumored to have made collections for the Newport, Kentucky mob. The Greek brothers sold it to another Greek relative, Alex Chaldekas, in 1974. Chaldekas had owned ABC Chili Parlor in Covington in the 1950s. Chaldekas held Arnold's only for two years before selling it to Jim Tarbell in 1976. Tarbell restored the upstairs dining rooms and bar to their current condition.

Current owner Ronda Androski worked for Tarbell for many years before buying him out in 1998. Her resilience has survived the aftermath of the 2001 riots and the recent economic slowdown.

Arnold's boasts an outdoor dining area with a stage that hosts live bands all throughout the year. It also has an infamous bathtub in the second-floor dining room, supposedly used for distilling bathtub gin. It has earned a reputation for good, tasty comfort food in a friendly atmosphere at moderate prices. One can enjoy a crab cake po' boy or a variety of burgers. Several nice pasta dishes, salads and chicken and waffles will certainly fill your belly for the evening. The Greek spaghetti pays homage to former owner Jim Christakos. Local beers on tap, imports and handcrafted specialty cocktails will help you enjoy your time at Arnold's.

By the early 1900s, some of Cincinnati's German watering holes had migrated south of the Rhine as German culture broke free of its enclave above the canal. One was Foucar's at 429 Walnut. It featured a rathskeller and offered free roast beef sandwiches at lunch that were accompanied by a purchased malted beverage. The focal point of its elaborate interior was *The Siesta*, a provocative female reclining nude painting by Covington artist Frank Duveneck. Mr. Foucar donated the painting to the art museum, saying, "That girl was too naked for my saloon, but not too naked for high society."

Another café south of Over-the-Rhine was the Bismarck Café, which first opened in about 1900 at 612 Vine Street. Run by Emil G. Schmitt, it became the largest establishment of its kind in Cincinnati and served the higher-class trade. By 1904, the café had relocated to 414 Walnut Street in the bottom floors of the Mercantile Building. It was known for its German food, and it featured separate gentlemen's and ladies' dining rooms, a rathskeller and a

The façade of Arnold's has not changed much since 1861. *Photo by author.*

staff of 150. The Bismarck served some of Cincinnati's favorite beers, from Hauck to Lackmann and Wiedemann Brewing, but also an import from Milwauke, Wisconsin: Pabst.

The inside of Foucar's Café, lined with German beer steins and buckheads. *Courtesy of the Public Library of Cincinnati and Hamilton County.*

The Gentlemen's Bar of the Bismarck Café. *Courtesy of the Public Library of Cincinnati and Hamilton County.*

The elegant interior of John Weber's café, with a showcase to the left of many cigars.
Courtesy of the Public Library of Cincinnati and Hamilton County.

The exterior of the Zinzinnati Café in its heyday, when it catered to German meatpackers of
Camp Washington. *Courtesy of the Public Library of Cincinnati and Hamilton County.*

John Weber had a café at 522 Vine that later was known as Alt Heidelberg Café. It was also a high-class spot and remained in business until the late 1950s, when it was rebranded as an Italian restaurant called the Isle of Capri, owned by the Palazzolo family. Schnitzel became veal parmesan, spaetzle became gnocchi and sweet Rhine wines became dry chiantis.

Cincinnati's German culture also spread up the hills, as German immigrants decided to leave the dirty downtown basin for the fresh air on the hills. Two well-known spots were in Walnut Hills. Schmiesing's Garden, started by Fred Schmiesing, was located near Gilbert and Blair Avenues, and not far away was Rosskopf's Biergarten. On the Westside, in the German neighborhood of Lick Run, there was Metz's Wine Garden, which ran from 1875 to 1919, and Gries' Wine Garden. Gries' was founded about 1865 by Charles Gries and sold in 1920 to become Quebec Gardens, which remained open into the 1990s, after it became a Chinese restaurant.

The Zinzinnati Café was once a haven for German meatpackers from the slaughterhouses in Camp Washington. Proprietor Heinrich Ludwig Mergard served draft Zinzinnati beer crafted by the Bellevue Brewery. The café was located at the corner of Colerain and Marshall and is now demolished. It had the same corner layout of the farmers' hotel in Northside and may have even been a farmers' hotel itself, given its vicinity to the old slaughterhouses.

In the Name of the Family, Not the Duchy

Mecklenburg Gardens, located on the corner of Highland and University Avenues, opened in 1865. Originally it was owned by John Neeb as the Mount Auburn Garden Restaurant and Billiard Saloon. Louis Mecklenburg, headwaiter for Neeb, bought the business in 1881 and renamed it in his honor. Lewis, with his son, Carl, ran the business for nearly fifty years.

In 1930, the Mecklenburgs turned the daily operations of the restaurant over to their headwaiter, George Reifenberger. George and his daughter, Mary Derrick, were the proprietors until 1966. By the mid-1960s, the trend to fine dining had begun to fade, and the restaurant began to decline and was sold to the first non-German owner, Joseph Sansone.

In 1974, the restaurant was reborn. New owner Scott Handey and chef Rob Fogel returned the establishment to its fine dining tradition, and it earned a Mobil four-star status. And in 1976, the historical 110-year-old building was listed on the National Register of Historic Places. Unfortunately

The exterior of Mecklenburg Gardens, taken from the corner of Highland and East University Avenues, looking northeast. *Courtesy of the Public Library of Cincinnati and Hamilton County.*

the rebirth was short-lived, and after several ownership changes and dining styles, mounting debt forced the restaurant to close its doors on New Year's Eve 1982.

It was reopened briefly as a pizza restaurant, but it was not until June 23, 1986, that new owners the Harten family reestablished Mecklenburg Gardens as a symbol of Cincinnati's German heritage. The place has been completely restored with a complete menu of German classics plus many American classics. It also serves one of the city's finest beer selections. Complete with an outdoor beer garden, a basement hall and an upstairs hall, today it hosts many German American clubs' meetings, like those of the Schlarraffia Society, the Handel's Mustard Club Monthly Brunches and the German American Citizen's League.

KNISH, KUGEL AND BLINTZ: JEWISH DELIS IN CINCINNATI

Considering its sizeable Jewish population, Cincinnati has suffered a deficit of good Jewish delis for far too long. Part of the problem is that there is no longer a distinct Jewish neighborhood in Cincinnati. The Jewish community moved together, first families and then the cultural institutions, nearly every thirty years. Starting in downtown East End, the community had moved to the West End by the Civil War. Around 1900, they started the ascent from the downtown basin to the hilltop suburbs of Walnut Hills and Avondale. Then they moved to Roselawn in the 1930s and to Golf Manor and Amberly Village in the 1950s. In the 1980s, they moved to Blue Ash, and today they are dispersed in the suburbs north of I-275.

But while there were still intact Jewish neighborhoods, Cincinnati had a diaspora of great New York–style Jewish delis, heavily influenced by Germanic and eastern European kosher delicacies.

One of the most famous Jewish delis in Cincinnati was Bilker's, operating for more than one hundred years. Founded in about 1900 by Polish immigrants George and Jenny Bilker on Central Avenue, it remained into the third generation and three locations, closing its Roselawn location in 2008. George and his wife opened at 5:00 a.m. so they could supply sandwiches for the factory workers on their way to work. Sometimes they wouldn't close until 1:00 a.m. or 2:00 a.m., until the last person was off the street. Rose Bilker Reis remembered standing on crates to reach the soda fountain. With the family living behind the store, Rose and her three sisters helped out regularly.

In its heyday, at its second location at Forest and Reading in Avondale, Bilker's was known throughout the city. It had fourteen delivery trucks and ten people taking telephone orders. The store's specialties were legend: pickles soaked in brine, with dill, garlic and spices; and hot corned beef brought steaming from the rear, sliced while its juice was still running and served on thick crusted rye bread. The store made its own mayonnaise and smoked its own fish, but its real distinction was its personalized service.

In 1953, when it moved from Avondale to Roselawn, it was a while before the business "took" in the new neighborhood, but with perseverance and an eye on quality, it was able to build the business back. The Bilkers worked tirelessly, with an eye to the next generation doing better.

Bilker's is famous for having KP coke, or Kosher for Passover—by dietary law, sweetened with sugar cane. So once a year for five or six weeks, you can buy Coke and Pepsi products made with sugar cane. For many who are not able to find sugar cane soda pop affordably or easily, it's exciting to have it available during Passover.

Izzy Cadets was founded in 1901 on Elm Street by Russian Jewish immigrants Izzy and Rose Cadets, who left a depression and oppressive czarist politics behind for a new life. Starting as a cook at the famous St. Nicholas Hotel, Izzy took his newly learned culinary confidence and started one of the first kosher-style delicatessens. The original location was described as a big city dive with its sloping floors. The emphasis was not on décor but

"EVERY YEAR FOR NEARLY HALF A CENTURY
BILKER'S HAS FEATURED MANISCHEWITZ!"

An ad from Bilker's, one of Cincinnati's longest-running Jewish delis, shows Nat Reis, the son-in-law of the founders, proudly displaying his kosher products. *Courtesy of Hebrew Union College Library.*

on the meat—pastrami, corned beef, smoked turkey and fresh chopped liver. Many remember the barrels of dill pickles at the Elm Street location and that it was truly kosher (no cheese) while Izzy ran it. Izzy would even put out different foods at Passover to comply with Jewish tradition.

Many people have strong memories of the stiff-necked and stubborn Izzy, likened to the character of the "Soup Nazi" on the TV sitcom *Seinfeld*. Izzy and his wife were famous for shouting back and forth between each other—no argument was too discreet for the public. Or people might remember that the price of food varied depending on what you were wearing and if you looked like you had extra money to spend. If you became a friend of Rose, she was known to put extra pickles and potato pancakes in your takeout order.

Their potato pancakes, although a side item, are still another favorite of their customers. Often called the best potato pancakes in the world, they are crispy on the outside, chewy on the inside, have just a hint of onion and are as big as a boxer's fist. Don't eat them in the car or without a napkin, as you'll probably find an embarrassing grease spot on your shirt or blouse.

Izzy's son, David, began running the restaurant in 1980. David shared many of his father's qualities, which allowed him to build the brand and business tremendously. In 1982, David opened a second restaurant on Sixth and Main Street in downtown Cincinnati, and he asked trusted friend John Geisen, then a skilled tradesman and a Catholic, to manage the location.

The Cadets family took John under their wing and began to instill in him their values. John came to understand that the secret to Izzy's success was rooted in offering superior quality along with the highest level of customer service. Together, John and David helped grow the business over the years, and John Geisen became the president and CEO.

With nine locations in the Tristate area, it has become another Cincinnati icon, where corned beef is king and sandwich making is high art. Known as the adoptive home of the reuben, it was certainly in business and serving famous corned beef before the two national restaurateurs given credit for its creation: Reuben Kulakofsky, a Lithuanian deli owner in Omaha, Nebraska, in the 1920s, and Arnold Reuben, German owner of Reuben's deli in New York City in 1912.

In addition to serving a goetta reuben, Izzy's serves signature sandwiches named after famous locals. The Jeff Ruby is a double-decker with rye bread, coleslaw, roast beef, turkey breast, chopped liver and Izzy's special dressing. The Peko is named after Cincinnati Bengal Domata Peko, who enjoys goetta, corned beef, provolone cheese and special sauce on a telera roll.

Temple Delicatessen and Sandwich shop, owned by the Zimmerman family, was on the west side of downtown at 130 West Seventh Street across from Shillito's Department Store. Founded in the late 1930s, it remained open until about 2006. A large three-tiered neon sign denoted its presence among a row of three- and four-story Italianate buildings on Seventh Street. It was a spacious place, offering immediate counter service in the front and immediate table service in the back. Temple featured super sandwiches and homemade soups, with hundreds of kosher food items, refrigerated cases of meats, cheeses, spreads, salads and lots of breads. Mr. Zimmerman had hard rolls, soft rolls, rounds, sesame-sprinkled rolls, garlic-laces, salted rolls, crisp rolls and tender rolls.

If you ate in, you could enjoy a pastrami on onion roll with a side of potato salad. Or you could feast on cheese blintzes, hot and light and sweet and smothered in sour cream or jelly. Mr. Zimmerman always had a poster advertising his signature rye bread, blazoned with the slogan, "You don't have to be Jewish to love Levy's Rye Bread!"

The Jewish community flocked to a New York–style deli in North Avondale called Loretta's in the 1960s and 1970s. Although she had some grocery items for sale, she concentrated mainly on table service. Loretta herself was a Catholic, but it was her sandwiches and coleslaw that attracted the Jewish community. King Records owner Syd Nathan was a regular at Loretta's. Her coleslaw was supposedly the best in town, made with a special mayonnaise from Louisville, Kentucky. One of Loretta's waitresses had a disagreement with Loretta and went to her competition—Stanley's Deli at Clinton Springs at Reading Road—but couldn't quite replicate her slaw.

Charles Pilder opened Pilder's Cafeteria downtown in 1928, when there were thirty-four kosher butchers downtown. After World War II, when they had moved to Avondale, there were twelve. When Charles's grandson, Danny Pilder, moved to Dillonvale, the store was the only kosher butcher in one hundred miles. They served brisket, roast chicken, noodle kugel, knishes, turkey chili and homemade soups. They pickled their corned beef on site and even had a "Frequent Fresser" card—which, when translated from the Yiddish, means "frequent snacker." Their last location was in Dillonwood Plaza at the corner of Galbraith and Plainfield Road.

The Upper Krust was owned in the 1960s by Meir Ovadia, an Israeli national and son-in-law of Mort Keller, owner of Sugar n' Spice. The Upper Krust was located on the east side of Reading Road between the Sycamore Square office and Porfidio's Wishing Well. It had a much broader appeal than the Jewish community because it would mix dairy and meat. And it served beer. It was less of a deli and more a well-stocked sandwich shop, famous for its high-rise sandwiches, with both corned beef and pastrami. Neither tornado nor robbery nor fire could stop the Upper Krust—only the owner's retirement. It took a major hit from the 1969 tornado but reopened. Ovadia, maybe believing that the original name had negative karma, changed it to Meir's Place. When he departed for Israel for the last time, a seafood restaurant called Sweeney's took over the building and was in operation for some ten to fifteen years.

BROADWAY MEETS BAVARIA IN MONFORT HEIGHTS AT FOREST VIEW GARDENS

Forest View Gardens, on the Westside in Monfort Heights, was a sixty-one-year-old tradition of "Broadway meets Bavaria." The place was known for its lively *gemutlichkeit*, with beer hall–style benches and tables in the showroom. Many fondly remember the Bavarian-style charm of the Edelweiss Dining Room, sparkling with lights and holiday greenery at Christmas. When it closed in 2000, then under the ownership of Trudie Seybold and her husband, Kurt, many patrons had been coming there for twenty years. It wasn't just the delicious and authentic German food that made people regular customers—it was the music sung by the servers. The servers, many of them students at the prestigious Cincinnati College Conservatory of Music (CCM), would drop their trays and sing show tunes and arias during service. Upon graduation, many would find musical careers all over the world.

Although the idea of the dinner/entertainment combination restaurant was Trudie's, her parents, both German natives, started the restaurant. Her father, Karl Klose, was an ironworker and her mother, Jennie, a cook. They met at the Citizenship House in Cincinnati. When they bought the rustic restaurant in the country in 1940, it joined other German restaurants in Cincinnati like Grammer's, Lenhardt's and Mecklenburg Gardens. During World War II, they avoided wartime rations because they raised their own beef and used vegetables from their own garden.

In 1975, Mrs. Klose broke her hip, and Trudie came back from Philadelphia, where she taught music, to run the restaurant with her two sons, Jay and Eddie. It was then that she had the idea of hiring servers who could sing. The rest is history. A unique German dinner/theater concept in Cincinnati was born. A hall of fame wall in the restaurant showed eight-by-ten glossy photos of former servers who went on to sing on Broadway or at other famous venues.

Kurt Seybold made a tradition of ending every evening at the restaurant by serenading customers, martini in hand, with his rendition of "My Way," written by Paul Anka and popularized by Frank Sinatra. Kurt Seybold was born in Memmingen, Germany, in 1937. Orphaned at a young age, he moved to Cincinnati at eighteen, sponsored by an aunt, and got his first job at Kahn's Meats, where many other German immigrants worked. He met his future wife at the restaurant while she was working for her parents. On the last night at the restaurant, Kurt changed the lyrics of his signature song to, "We did it our way."

German Hungarian in Clifton

Always described as a German restaurant, Lenhardt's actually traces its roots back to Kikinda, Yugoslavia, now part of Serbia, where its founders, brothers Anton and Kristoff Lenhardt, were born. Many left Yugoslavia in the 1950s to escape the Communist regime, but the Lenhardt family left Kikinda for Austria after the Second World War to escape the Russians, who turned their town into a forced labor camp. But it was Hollywood that brought the extended Lenhardt family to the United States and to Cincinnati. Tony Lenhardt, son of Kristoff and Anni, arrived in Cincinnati in March 1950 with his mother to film the movie *Here Comes the Groom*, which headlined Bing Crosby and Anna Maria Alberghetti. While he was attending grade school, Toni was selected to portray one of the refugee children in the movie. The rest of the family arrived in Cincinnati on December 23, 1951. Anton and his wife, Emmi, followed in 1953.

Anton and his brother, Kristoff, opened their first Lenhardt's restaurant in 1955 at 2011 West McMillan. With only twelve seats, the restaurant expanded quickly, and in 1963, Anton Lenhardt purchased the Goetz House, located at 151 West McMillan. Famous Cincinnati beer baron Christian Moerlein had given the house to his daughter, Lizzie, and her husband, John Goetz Jr., in 1891 on their tenth wedding anniversary.

Kristoff Lenhardt would split with his brother and open his own Lenhardt's restaurant on Reading Road in the 1970s, where he specialized in Viennese tortes, as well as another restaurant, Lenhardt's Chateau Combi, on State Street in Mount Washington.

Anton and Emmi retired in 1977, leaving the business to their daughter and son-in-law, Erika and William "Joe" Windholtz. Frau Windholtz was always very generous in giving free dinner coupons for raffles and fundraisers at the University of Cincinnati. Joe and Erika retired in 2000, leaving the restaurant to their daughter, Christy Windholtz Lammers. She had run Christy's Rathskellar, the basement bar, famous for its shelves of German beer steins and as being one of the only places in Cincinnati to get Warsteiner beer on tap. Christy's was a popular hangout for UC students. The Rathskellar hosted a weekly *stammtisch* where students could practice their German vocabulary. Christy later added an outdoor beer garden that was popular with students.

The Hungarian influence was seen at Lenhardt's in menu items like the favorite chicken paprikash, Hungarian goulash and liver dumplings. Lenhardt's also served three Cincinnati favorites not native to Germany or Hungary: sauerkraut balls, Glier's goetta and hot slaw. Additionally, it served the familiar *S*s of any good German fare—schnitzel, sauerbraten, spaetzle and strudel. Offering eleven schnitzels, Lenhardt's served the most varieties of schnitzel of any German restaurant in Cincinnati. Schnitzel is a slice of prime-quality veal, trimmed of all fat, pounded thin, breaded and pan fried. Wienerschnitzel was the standard, without any sauce, but Lenhardt's served varieties like the jaeger or hunter schnitzel, topped in a brown sauce flavored with mushroom and bacon.

The now demolished Lenhardt's German Hungarian Restaurant, originally a gift from beer baron Christian Moerlein to his daughter, Lizzie. *Courtesy of Don Prout, Cincinnati Views.*

Lenhardt's Veal Specialties

Every Meal Prepared to Order, Allow 10 to 30 Minutes

Don't say you have never liked "VEAL." Try any one of our "SCHNITZELS" and you will be amazed by the difference!

	Dinner
WIENER SCHNITZEL is a slice of veal dipped into egg and home-made bread crumbs and fried to a golden brown	$2.80
SCHNITZEL au NATUREL is served in its own juice	2.80
SCHNITZEL a la PARISIENNE is dipped into one egg and fried so that the coating has the appearance of the fluffiest of French omelets	2.90
SCHNITZEL a la HOLSTEIN named after Count Holstein, is prepared the same as a Wiener Schnitzel but served with a Fried Egg on the top and Anchovies	3.00
SAILOR SCHNITZEL, au NATUREL to which has been added a slice of fried Ham and a slice of melted pure Swiss Cheese	3.00
THE HUNGARIAN PAPRIKA SCHNITZEL to which Onions and Paprika are added to make the Hungarian Pusta come right to your table	3.00
KAISER SCHNITZEL, au NATUREL served in a delicate cream sauce to which Lemon Rind and Capers have been added. Truly a Gourmet's Delight	3.00
ITALIAN SCHNITZEL again a Wiener Schnitzel which has been prepared with Parmesan Cheese and just a soupcon of Garlic	3.00
RAHMSCHNITZEL — a Naturschnitzel to which has been added finely crumbled lean sugar-cured bacon and chopped onion and which has been bubbling in pure sweet cream	3.10
ST. MORITZ SCHNITZEL Swiss Chalet, breaded veal filet stuffed with Ham, Gruyere Cheese	3.30

"What Is A Schnitzel?"

A Schnitzel is a slice of prime quality milk-fed Veal, cut in our own kitchen, trimmed of all fat and sinew, beaten and fried. This holds true for all types of Schnitzel.

Sauerbraten	with Potato Pancake and Applesauce. Sauerbraten is marinated beef roast, a famous German dish	2.70
Kassler Rippchen	Pork Loin marinated and smoked, then roasted and served with sauerkraut and mashed potatoes	2.30

T-BONE STEAK — Vegetable and Salad	3.30
ROAST TOP ROUND OF BEEF — Gravy, Mashed Potatoes and Salad	2.40
GRILLED PORK CHOPS — French Fries, Applesauce	2.50
GRILLED GROUND ROUND STEAK — French Fries, Salad	2.40
PAN-FRIED CHICKEN — (Fried to order), Potatoes and Salad	2.50
OMELET — Bacon, Western, Jelly, Cheese or Ham, Potatoes and Salad	2.10

Dessert	Home Made Vienna and Hungarian Torte, Apple or Cherry Strudel .40		a la mode .15 add.
	Hungarian Palatschinken with Apricot Preserve .50		
	Home Made Pie .30	Cream Pie .40	Ice Cream .30

Special Sandwiches

CLUB SANDWICH — (open face)	1.40	**FISH SANDWICH** — Cole Slaw, French Fries	.90
HOT ROAST BEEF SANDWICH — Gravy, Mashed Potatoes, Cole Slaw	1.10	**CHEESEBURGER DE LUXE**	.80
OYSTER SANDWICH — Cole Slaw, French Fries	1.00	**HAMBURGER DE LUXE**	.70
SHRIMP SALAD	1.50	**EPICUREAN SALAD**	1.50

The 1962 menu from Lenhardt's shows the number of different schnitzels it served. *Courtesy of the Public Library of Cincinnati and Hamilton County.*

The restaurant closed in December 2013. After much dissent from the Cincinnati Preservation Association and Clifton neighbors, the new buyers razed the beautiful, historic building in January 2014 to build more student condos.

Hungarian Rhapsoday

A bit outside of the city to the east in Newtown, another German-Hungarian restaurant has been open since 1973. Laszlo's Iron Skillet was founded by another set of Austro-Hungarian escapees from the Communist regime, Laszlo and Elizabeth Molnar.

In 1956, a popular uprising in Hungary was brutally suppressed by the Soviet Union, and 200,000 Hungarians fled the country, among them Laszlo Molnar Sr., then eighteen. He got to Austria and then to the United States, to a job on a farm in Indiana.

Molnar found support from the few Hungarians who were in Cincinnati. He worked for a time at Lenhardt's in Clifton, also owned by Austro-Hungarian immigrants. That's where he met the woman who became his wife in 1962, Elizabeth Herbai. She was also from the same small town as Molnar, Se, near Szombathely in western Hungary.

Over the years, Molnar worked his way up in the restaurant business. He worked at Zimmer's in Oakley, the Colony, downtown and at the Hearth in Mount Carmel. After those experiences, he had become a seasoned chef and decided to break out on his own.

In 1971, Molnar bought a lunch counter and café called the Iron Skillet in Mount Washington. He served standard sandwiches and lunch counter fare, but he put his crepes on the menu, too. In 1973, he moved to the current building at Valley Avenue and Newtown Road and turned it into a small café serving both Hungarian and American dishes.

His children, Laszlo Jr. and Monica Lippmeier, grew up working in the restaurant, and it was they who inherited the business when their father retired in 1989. With a history as rich as some of its foods, Laszlo's has survived escaping the Communists, a fire, a flood and forty years in business.

Traditional Hungarian and German specialties form the basis of the menu. The German influence is seen in its offering of ten types of schnitzel, including a newly invented Cincinnati schnitzel topped with goetta and pepper sauce; sauerbraten; and the requisite Cincinnati sauerkraut balls, among other dishes.

The Hungarian influence can be seen in its three types of goulash, chicken and steak paprikash, stuffed cabbage and Hortobagyi crepes, light and spongy crepes filled with shredded goulash pork and topped with sour cream sauce.

In 2013, a fire burned the Valley Avenue location, and it is now operating out of a former Thai restaurant in a strip mall on Main Street in Newtown, contemplating its next move.

THE BLACK FOREST

In the suburbs of Westchester Township, the Black Forest served German fare with a Bavarian overtone. Owner George Fraundorfer and wife Christel started a restaurant in 1964 in Monfort Heights called the Gaslight and then took over the Black Forest on Colerain Avenue, which was in an old Red Carpet Motel. Fraundorfer moved it to its last cozy spot on Route 42 in 1983. The manager, Neil Gilman, has worked for him since 1967.

Fraundorfer hailed from the small town of Garmisch-Partnekirchen in the Bavarian Alps, where he was a fourth-generation restaurateur. His family still operates a *gasthof* there. Fraundorfer had served for six years as sous chef at the Maisonette before going off on his own.

Inside the Black Forest, Oktoberfest never ended. The interior was what you might find in places in Germany's Schwartzwald or the real Black Forest—exposed beams and cuckoo clocks. You could drink beer in large glass boots and hear oom-pah music being played by accordians. There were four rooms. The main dining room had a cozy fireplace and a dance floor. There was a Jaeger Room, or Hunt Room, with buckheads and German whiskey decanters on display. There was a beerstube and a Bavarian room. Outside, the restaurant looked like an overgrown Bavarian cottage.

The food was all the German/Bavarian/Cincinnati food you would expect: sauerkraut balls, German eggrolls, Oktoberfest rotisserie chicken, pork roast and sauerkraut, wienerschnitzel, sauerbraten and rindrouladen. In the earlier days, the Black Forest had a fish tank from which it served fresh whole trout almondine.

Without a lot of advertising power, it relied on the patronage of all the German clubs in Cincinnati and festivals like Taste of Cincinnati and Oktoberfest to get its name in front of people.

In 2006, longtime manager Neil Gilman took over with plans of updating the interior and exterior to cater to a female clientele—

landscaping, updating the bathrooms and smaller plates and more desserts. However, his plans fell right in the middle of the recession, and the restaurant closed in 2009.

Black Forest Hasenpfeffer

5-pound rabbit, cut in pieces
½ cup vinegar
½ cup water
1 cup red wine
1 large onion, diced
10 peppercorns
4 juniper berries
1 bay leaf
4 cloves
4 tablespoons bacon fat
4 tablespoons flour
salt and pepper

Place rabbit pieces in a bowl. In saucepan combine vinegar, water, red wine, onion, peppercorns, juniper berries, bay leaf and cloves. Simmer over low heat for 10 minutes. Pour this over rabbit and marinate in refrigerator for two days.

Heat the bacon fat in a casserole and add rabbit. Brown on all sides, sprinkling with flour. Stir over medium heat until flour is brown. Strain the marinade and add to the warmed rabbit. Cover and simmer for 45 minutes. Add salt and pepper to taste. Serve with spaetzle.

THE LAST TRUE GERMAN WORKINGMAN'S SALOON IN OVER-THE-RHINE

In 1999, Stenger's Café, the last of the German workingman's saloons, closed in Over-the-Rhine. A sign of the times for the neighborhood, its owner, Leo Sunderman, had been serving German food there since 1947. When he returned from a tour of duty in World War II, he took over from his father-in-law, John Stenger Jr., who had opened the café in 1934. For more than sixty-five years, Stenger's had been an urban magnet, attracting clientele from downtown, uptown and the suburbs. At any lunchtime, you could see lawyers, judges, winos, professors and city workers eating together. Local celebrities like Buddy LaRosa and Pete Rose used to come to Stenger's.

Sunderman's menu was famous for his homemade sauerbraten, mock turtle soup, meatloaf and other specialties. And as the dusty Hudy Gold sign behind the bar advertised, all could be washed down with a cold mug of our local favorite beer. Some came for the coconut cream pie or the open-faced roast beef sandwiches. But the blue plate specials that time forgot made the fare affordable to the blue-collar workingman. Monday's special was spare ribs and sauerkraut, Tuesday's was sauerbraten, Thursday's was fried pork chops and Friday's was fried fish for the observant Catholics.

Sunderman sold in 1999 to restaurateur Doug Bootes, who hired Paul Sebron, the manager of Mr. Pig in Findlay Market, to manage Stenger's for him. By 2001, there were signs of life showing from the new Stenger's. Sebron hosted very successful crayfish nights. But then the April 2001 riots erupted in the streets of Over-the-Rhine, quickly slashing sales and forcing him to close. Stenger's Café is a piece of German history now lost.

Chapter 3

CHILITOWN, USA

There's no other food that Cincinnatians go crazy for more than Cincinnati-style chili. It's created the Chili Wars between the two largest chain chili parlors, Skyline and Gold Star. Although it's not really true that there is nothing like Cincinnati chili anywhere else in the world, it is true about the threeway, which was invented here, on Vine Street at the Empress Chili Parlor. But it was the Coney Island that brought what would become Cincinnati-style chili to Cincinnati. Most people think that Texas-style chili—the typical "bowl of red"—migrated north and somehow morphed into Cincinnati chili. But it was the Macedonians and, later, Greeks who immigrated through New York City who brought their *saltsa kima*, which means "meat sauce," with them as they migrated with the railroads and other jobs in the upper Midwest.

These immigrants saw their countrymen running Coney Island stands as soon as they stepped off the boat at the New York amusement park from which they took their name. They saw the sauce, with which they were familiar, being used as almost a condiment on the top. But to avoid sounding too ethnic, they borrowed the familiar name of "chili," even though it has no ancestral roots in American chili. And thus a quintessential American food icon, the Coney Island, was born.

As Macedonian and Greek immigrants migrated through the Midwest, they took their Coney Island, with its meat sauce, and modified it to their new regions. Those who settled around Detroit found great success with the Coney Island as a convenience food for the automotive working class. Today, there are more than five hundred Coney Island shops around Detroit. Those who settled in Pennsylvania and New York used what they call a Texas red hot, a spicier hot dog, and topped it with meat sauce and onions. As it made its way through West Virginia and the Carolinas, they adapted it even more by adding coleslaw to the top, creating the slaw dog. It even made it into London in Laurel County, Kentucky, with the chili bun, a version of the Coney Island without the hot dog.

Then, in 1922, the Coney Island landed in Cincinnati with the Kiradjieff brothers, Athanas and Ivan, who opened the first Cincinnati chili parlor, called the Empress, inside the Empress burlesque theater on Vine Street. They added their Turkish/Middle Eastern spice blend, the *baharat*, to the *saltsa kima* to create a unique flavor for their Coney Islands, which initially were naked—without cheese. But unlike their other immigrant brothers, they innovated. They took the meat sauce, now called chili, and added it to spaghetti, creating a new dish they called chili spaghetti or chili mac. Then, in the 1930s, when one customer suggested they add shredded cheddar cheese to the chili spaghetti, the threeway

Co-owner Ivan Kiradjieff smiles proudly behind the counter of the original Empress Chili location in the 1920s. *Courtesy of John Kiradjieff.*

A 1973 photo showing the second Empress Chili location on Fifth Street. Next to the chili parlor was a Sixty Second Shop. *Courtesy of John Kiradjieff.*

was born. At another's request, they then added it to the Coney Island, and the Cincinnati cheese coney was born. And that's what started a movement. This new convenience food, which seemed truly American, swept through the city and created what is now a more than $250 million industry, with more than 250 chili parlors.

The Kiradjieff brothers were very helpful in setting up their immigrant countrymen in the chili business. They trained them on how to run and operate and where to set up shop. Many former Empress Chili employees went on to start their own chili parlors. Athanas's association with a local bank was instrumental in getting fellow countrymen loans.

The two largest chains in the city, Skyline and Gold Star, came along nearly thirty years after the founding of the first, Empress Chili. Skyline came along in 1949 in East Price Hill, started by Nicholas Lambrinides, a former worker at Empress and immigrant from Kastoria, Greece. Gold Star came along in 1965, founded in Mount Washington by four Jordanian immigrant brothers: Fahhad, Fahid, Basheer and Beshara Daoud. They bought Hamburger Heaven and its chili recipe from Thomas Manoff, whose family had owned several chili parlors in Cincinnati and northern Kentucky before. Both recipes are traced to the original Empress.

The real story of the growth of Cincinnati chili lies with all the independent chili parlors around town that preceded the two big chains. They are the

EMPRESS CHILI
Athanas "Tom" and Ivan "John" Kiradjieff,
Downtown Cincinnati, Vine St. (1922)

DIXIE CHILI
*Nick Sarakatsanis
& Petro Manoff*
Newport, KY (1929)

CAMP WASHINGTON CHILI
Steve Andon & Zambrus
Camp Washington (1940)

CHILI TIME
Peter & Harry Vidas
St. Bernard (1943)

STRAND CHILI PARLOR
Petro & Thomas Manoff
Newport, KY (1931)

CRYSTAL CHILI
Tom Sarakatsanis
Newport, KY (1946)

UNCLE STEVE'S (U.S CHILI)
John Storgion
Colerain Township (1977)

COVINGTON CHILI
*Christy Terzieff
(1936) Steven &
Thelma Andon
Stephens (1950s)*

OAKLEY CHILI
George Manoff (1936)

LIBERTY CHILI
James & Menca Peterson
Northside (1938)

TIP TOP HAMBURGERS
*Thomas Manoff & Frank Bedell
(1946)*

PARK CHILI
Norman Bazoff
Northside (1937)

CHEVIOT CHILI
*James & Menca Peterson
(1940s)*

HAMBURGER HEAVEN
Thomas Manoff (1947)

MANOFF'S RANCHO BURGER
Thomas Manoff
Santa Cruz, CA (1959)

GOLD STAR CHILI
Fahid, Basheer, Beshara, Fahhad Daoud (1965)

THE SILVER SPUR
Art Marsh,
Santa Cruz, CA (1965)

THE CHILI HOUSE
Fahid Daoud
Jordan (1984)

VINYL / DINER ON SYCAMORE
Roula Daoud
Over-the-Rhine (2006)

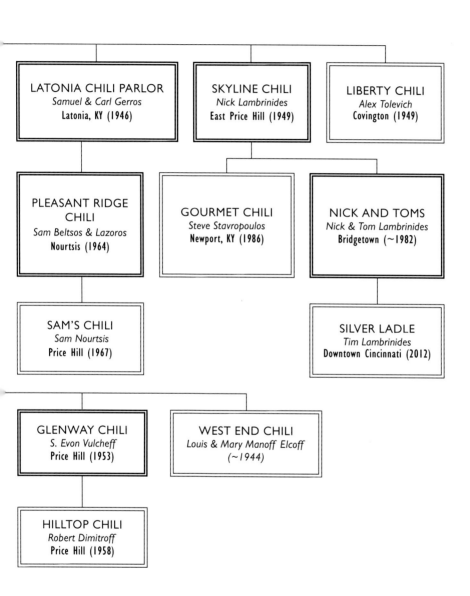

FIGURE 1. The Cincinnati chili family tree, showing how other chili parlors grew from former Empress employees.

A 1950s photo showing the inside of Hamburger Heaven before being sold to the Daoud brothers of Gold Star. *Courtesy of the Manoff family.*

ones that laid the groundwork for the ability to franchise. They served their local neighborhoods and got the "chili crave" implanted in their respective areas of the city.

The first other chili parlor to open in downtown Cincinnati was Paul Taleff's Famous Chili Parlor in 1929 at 601 West Sixth Street. Taleff would operate his chili parlor until the mid-1950s and employ his family, who also opened other restaurants.

By 1946, more than half a dozen other chili parlors graced downtown. There was Main Chili Kitchen at 22 East Sixth Street, owned by William Gaz. Chili Kitchen had dual locations at 2509 Gilbert Avenue and 607 Walnut Street. Cincinnati Chili Inc. at 639 Vine was run by Fay Snapps, Dalton Chandler and Leonard Lipshutz. Tom's Chili Parlor at 1535 Central Avenue was run by Theresa Driviakis. B&M Chili Parlor at 3200 Colerain Avenue was a partnership between George Perdikakis, Charles Balli and Steve Moraites. Charles and Art Sarakatsannis ran the Crystal Grill at 244 West McMicken near the Imperial Theatre. By 1953, a total of eighteen chili parlors were dotting downtown. The Court Street Chili Parlor, West End Chili Parlor, Main and Liberty Chili, the Empire Chili Parlor and George's Chili Parlor were new additions.

Brack Sizemore owned and operated the Mohawk Chili Parlor from about 1957 into the early 1960s, across from the Empire Theatre in Over-the-Rhine. He got his Cincinnati-style chili recipe from Lou Haritopoulos, his manager at the Paradise Coffee Shop and Chili Parlor at Eighth and State in Price Hill, owned by Sam Haggis.

It didn't take long for chili to move out of downtown. In 1936, the Oakley Chili Parlor, owned by George and Mary Manoff, was feeding theater customers. They sold in 1938 to Norman Bazoff, who would open Park Chili in Northside across from the Park Theater. The Liberty Chili Parlor opened in 1939 in the old Liberty Theatre in Northside. In 1940, a new movie theater, the 20th Century, opened in Oakley, and then the 20th Century Chili Shop opened, operated by Catherine and John Pashal. One corner in Oakley at Madison Avenue and Appleton Street housed a chili parlor for more than thirty years—Shorty's Chili Kitchen, owned by Frank B. Knefel, became the Chili Company, which closed in 2009.

Our famous James Beard Award–winning chili parlor, Camp Washington Chili, was founded by Steve Andon in 1940, when meatpackers and factory workers dominated its lunchtime and late-night crowds. His nephew, Johnny Johnson, took over and currently runs the iconic spot with his wife and daughter.

Cincinnati chili had reached Norwood by 1946. Three chili parlors—Carl's Chili Kitchen, the Emperor Chili Parlor and the Norwood Chili Parlor, all on Montgomery Road—fed Norwood natives, GM employees and Xavier University students.

Chili parlors had reached St. Bernard by the 1940s. Pandelis "Pete" Vidas opened the first Chili Time Restaurant in 1943 on Vine Street in St. Bernard. Vidas had emigrated from Variko, Greece. He first opened across the street from his current restaurant at 4720 Vine Street and then operated a second location at 7500 Reading Road in Bond Hill. In 1946, William E. Williams was operating the X-L Chili Parlor at 6006 Vine Street.

By the 1960s, Cincinnati chili parlors had been around for nearly four decades. Several chili parlors had moved up Reading Road and Vine Street to the neighborhoods of Reading and Elmwood Place, respectively. Reading had the Chili Bowl at 6100 Vine Street, Cretan's Chili Restaurant at 7039 Vine Street and Vince's Chili Kitchen at 6014 Vine Street.

The Chili Bowl in Elmwood Place was a long-running independent chili parlor. Started in 1938 on Vine Street in the first floor of a house, its motto

The exterior of Park Chili Parlor in Northside, Cincinnati's oldest continually operating chili parlor location. *Author's collection.*

was "Chili the 'way' you like it." Sylvan Kahn bought the parlor in 1973 and moved to Cincinnati. Kahn opened two more Chili Bowl locations, one downtown and one in Reading, but the Elmwood Place location, being close to P&G, did the best business. Vince's Chili Kitchen down the block was

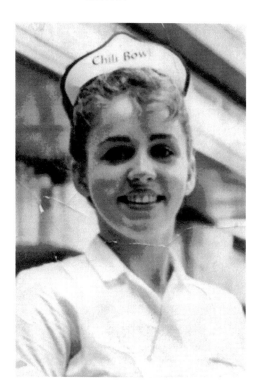

Right: This smiling beauty worked at the Chili Bowl in Elmwood Place during the 1950s. *Courtesy of Bill Kahn.*

Below: This small walk-up, Sam's Chili, has been serving Price Hill chili fans since 1967. *Author's collection.*

FISH • CHICKEN • CHILI • GYROS • PIZZA

competition but never really took away any business from the Chili Bowl. He sold in the 1980s and went into the funeral business.

Other locations still operating popped up in the 1960s. Pleasant Ridge Chili founder Tony Sideris, from Kastoria, Greece, found a great location on Montgomery Road in 1964, next to the old Ridge Theatre. Blue Ash Chili was founded in 1968 by Theodore Christopoulos and was later featured on *Diners, Drive-Ins and Dives*.

The Westside of Cincinnati became known for its "Chili Highway," Glenway Avenue, which has a chili parlor about every mile of its eight-mile length. Starting with the Price Hill Skyline, there's also Sam's Chili, Price Hill Chili, a Westwood Skyline, a Western Hills Gold Star, J&J Restaurant and a Bridgetown Empress Chili. Sam's Chili was founded in 1967 by Sam Nourtsis, son of the co-founder of Price Hill Chili. Famous for its coneys, it has a few tables and is more of a walk-up and carryout than a dine-in. Price Hill, founded in 1960 by Sam Beltsos and father-in-law Lazarus Nourtsis, is a neighborhood icon that has hosted presidents and other politicians. J&J Restaurant was founded in 1964 by Jim Mintsoulos and John Asilov.

Thomas Manoff, founder of Hamburger Heaven, said about the Westside of Cincinnati that you couldn't roll your window down without smelling chili wafting from some direction. A Covedale Chili Parlor and a Crookshank Chili operated near Glenway Avenue for many years. A Westside Chili Parlor operated on Glenway Avenue until recently, offering other varieties of chili in addition to Cincinnati style.

Pete Poulos opened his first Chili Company restaurant in 1978 in White Oak. By 1984, he had twelve locations throughout Cincinnati. Leveraging a poor economy in the early 1980s, Poulos acquired locations of other failed restaurants cheaply and got great discounts on equipment packages. His goal was to open up one hundred locations within one hundred miles of Greater Cincinnati, but quick growth prevented him from meeting these goals, and the chain went defunct.

Mount Adams had two chili parlors in the 1960s. Joyce Middendorf and her husband, David Middendorf, a former left guard with the Bengals in the late 1960s, owned the Red Onion Chili Parlor until 1968. Another chili parlor, Lovebirds, occupied the space that is now Teak Thai Restaurant in the 1960s. Mount Adams is one of the only neighborhoods in Cincinnati that does not have a chain chili parlor.

Even the far Eastside area Madeira has its JK's Chili, founded in 1973 on Laurel Avenue in a small strip center. Its interior has a six-stool counter, a handful of tables and a row of booths along the wall. Along with the

The Sunset Chili parlor was the last to inhabit the original Empress location before it was razed. *Courtesy of Hamilton County Auditor.*

traditional chili, it serves breakfast, double-deckers and fried sandwiches. Known for its four-coneys-for-five-dollars deal, it's a pleasant indie that's lasted through the Big 2 franchising.

In the 1980s, the short-lived Markets International Mall in Tricounty had a chili parlor called Olympic Chili and Tater Shack that offered coneys; 3, 4 and 5 Way Chili; and tater tots with a variety of toppings, including Cincinnati chili. A Cincinnati chili–topped plate of tater tots is a concept that hasn't been commercialized before or since Olympic Chili!

Only a few chili parlors have veered off the sacred menu to create new menu items. Gold Star has made the Oktoberfest coney with the addition of sauerkraut and a Cincinnati brat instead of a hot dog to the cheese coney. Skyline has created a Cincinnati chili burrito. You can also see a goetta dog cheese coney at some of the various Goettafests in the city. In homage to the hometown chili, Husman's makes a Cincinnati chili–flavored potato chip. In 2015, local brewers Blank Slate Brewing Company teamed up with Colorado's Oskar Blues Brewery to make a Cincinnati chili–flavored porter—spicing the barley with cumin, coriander, allspice and cinnamon and then smoking it.

At ninety-three years old, the formula for Cincinnati chili is still a secret. Many falsely believe that it contains chocolate. There are nearly 250 chili parlors—125 for Skyline, 90 for Gold Star and 25 independents. But the hundreds of small independent parlors paved the way for the big chains' success. The format remains nearly the same as it did that cool fall day on October 22, 1922, when the Kiradjieff brothers opened the first chili parlor. Our love and enthusiasm for our hometown chili will probably not change in the next ninety-three years, either.

Chapter 4
THE RISE OF FAST FOOD IN CINCINNATI

In Cincinnati, before McDonald's was everywhere, many local burger and fast-food brands thrived. Before the 1950s, fast food was only available in downtown areas and bustling entertainment districts late at night. Cincinnati got its first White Castle restaurant in 1927, one of the first cheap fast-food concepts in the country. There were a small number of family-style restaurants, lunch counters and fine dining restaurants. The majority of Cincinnatians chose to eat at home, and the highway system that would lend growth to fast food was not widely developed until the 1960s.

The strategy of fast food was to choose locations that were high traffic to produce the most sales. Early on, these were the old turnpikes and main thoroughfares, like Reading Road and Central Parkway, that existed before the modern highway systems of the 1960s were built.

In Cincinnati, the first true fast-food entrepreneurs were the Macedonian chili parlor owners like the Kiradjieff brothers. They set up a formula in the 1920s for picking chili parlor locations near movie theaters that lasted for decades. This was to get foot traffic and late-night entertainment crowds. Nearly every chili parlor that opened in Cincinnati between 1922 and 1950 was placed near a movie theater.

Drugstores like Walgreens and Dow Drugs had extensive menus at their lunch counters, which also featured soda fountains. Some dairies in town had their own dairy bars with soda fountains, which were popular hangouts for high school kids. Those fast-food locations that did exist were predominantly "carhops." These types of places, like Webbies in

This 1965 Walgreens lunch counter menu shows its large selection of items. *Courtesy of the Public Library of Cincinnati and Hamilton County.*

An ad for West Pharmacy on Glenway Avenue showing the atmosphere of Cincinnati drugstore soda fountains. *Courtesy of the Price Hill Historical Society.*

Roselawn or Jerry's Drive-In on Springfield Pike in Woodlawn, were places that had limited seating inside and instead offered outside car service, with radio-ordering kiosks carside.

Around the same time that McDonald's came to Cincinnati, Burger Chef had opened locations on the Westside of Cincinnati. Founded in 1957 in Indianapolis, Indiana, by Frank and Donald Thomas, Burger Chef had the Big

4028 HARRISON

"World's Greatest

Hamburger"

A 1960s Burger Chef ad showing the workings of the Western Hills location. *Courtesy of the Price Hill Historical Society.*

Chef double burger and a Super Chef quarter-pounder hamburger. It also had a works bar where customers could add their own toppings on their burgers. Another innovation that Burger Chef introduced was its Funmeal, or kids' meal, in the early 1970s, with toys and stories to build the brand with young customers. When McDonald's introduced its kids' meal in 1979, Burger Chef sued but lost. Burger Chef sold to Hardee's in 1999, and the brand went defunct.

The first McDonald's franchise came to Cincinnati in 1959, under the ownership of Lou Groen, the man who would invent the Filet-O-Fish sandwich to satisfy his Cincinnati Catholic customers on Friday. One day, while working in his father-in-law's Cincinnati restaurant, Groen was leafing through *Restaurant Management* magazine when he spotted a few advertisements for franchise opportunities. He saw a tiny ad for McDonald's fifteen-cent hamburgers.

When Groen answered the ad, he was told that $950 would buy him exclusive McDonald's franchise rights in Ohio, Kentucky, Indiana and parts of Pennsylvania. But he didn't have that much money. So he invested a few hundred dollars in a district franchise that included Greater Cincinnati and northern Kentucky. He opened his first store in 1959.

Groen struggled his first few years to build the McDonald's brand in Cincinnati. Business was especially bad in the largely Catholic community on Fridays. Before the Second Vatican Council in 1965, Catholics abstained from meat *every* Friday, not just during Lent. Rather than get a burger, his customers were going to Frisch's Big Boy because it served fish sandwiches. So Groen devised his Filet-O-Fish prototype in 1961.

He proposed it to Ray Kroc, CEO of McDonald's, who didn't like the idea of fish stinking up his restaurants. But Kroc made a deal. He had an idea for a new sandwich himself, called the Hula burger, which had a slice of pineapple and a slice of cheese. So Kroc waged that on Good Friday of 1962, the Hula Burger and Filet-O-Fish would be released simultaneously on select menus, and whichever sold the most would become a menu item. Kroc's idea sold about 6, while Groen's fish sandwich sold 350.

McDonald's introduced the Filet-O-Fish in 1963 in an aggressive campaign against Frisch's. The Filet-O-Fish would become a cash cow for McDonald's and would help Groen build forty-three franchise locations in Cincinnati with three thousand employees and annual sales of $60 million.

Frisch's current VP of marketing, Karen Meier, said that the need for McDonald's to create the Filet-O-Fish was the tipping point that launched Frisch's from a successful brand to an iconic brand.

In 1954, the Bresler's Ice Cream Company expanded into the fast-food market. Company executives were looking for a new outlet to promote higher sales of their malts and shakes without altering the existing Bresler's brand. Under the name Henry's Hamburgers, a large number of franchises were established. They were named after Henry Bresler, one of the founding brothers of the ice cream enterprise. In just two years, Bresler's had thirty-five locations in Chicago, and by the early 1960s, there were more than two hundred locations across the company. Its neon sign with its smiling burger shined in Cincinnati at two locations: one in Finneytown on Winton Road, on a site that a McDonald's would take over and operate for more than thirty years, and one in Oakley. Kids loved Bresler's fifteen-cent hamburgers and its fries. Active in the early 1960s, it operated for a brief time under the brand Barney's before shutting down completely.

Another competitor was the Sixty Second Shops, which was a clone of the already established Frisch's. Like Frisch's, it had a double-patty sandwich, called the Big 60, with a pinkish thousand island type of special sauce. But unlike Frisch's, it was open twenty-four hours. Cincinnati had locations downtown on Fifth across from the Greyhound station, next to Empress Chili, on North College Hill on Goodman Avenue, at Peebles' Corner in Walnut Hills, in Mount Washington, in Hartwell at the southeast corner of Compton and Vine and in Silverton on Montgomery Road near Graftons.

Another local clone of Sixty Second Shop was the Tick Tock Sandwich shop, which located near streetcar transfer stops and catered to those wanting a quick, convenient bite before catching their next transfer. One location was at 204 McMillen in Clifton near the University of Cincinnati.

It's a delicious "BIG SIXTY" the BEST double-decker Hamburger served... ANYWHERE! SIXTY SECOND SHOPS, Inc. Open 24 Hours a Day

A Sixty Second Shop ad promoting its Big Sixty double-decker burger. *Courtesy of St. Margaret Mary Catholic Church.*

The Parkmoor was a Frisch's drive-up clone, headquartered out of Dayton, that had locations in Reading and Summit. Its feature burger was called the King Burger. It also served Dixie Famous Fried Chicken.

Carter's was yet another local hamburger place that also promoted the Kentucky Fried Chicken Original Recipe along with its hamburgers. It had several locations in the 1950s and 1960s, including Kennedy Heights on Montgomery Road.

Golden Point Hamburgers, a Chicago chain founded in 1958, had several locations in Cincinnati, with its famous A-frame building with walk-up service. One location was at Northbrook near Mount Healthy. At this

Parkmoor

JUMBO BURGER

Two bigger and better patties of pure beef on toasted bun, with melted American cheese, crisp lettuce, pickles and our own special Jumbo sauce **.55**

SANDWICHES

HAMBURGER, Pure fresh beef we grind daily. Big, juicy patty .... .30
DeLUXE HAMBURGER, Served with crisp lettuce, tomato slice, our own sauce .... .35
PARKY STEAK SANDWICH, Tender, grilled chopped sirloin steak on toasted bun, sweet
  Bermuda onion and sauce if desired .... .55

OCEAN WHITEFISH .... **.55**
Two tender juicy fillets of ocean white fish, served with lettuce and tangy tartar sauce on toasted bun.

THE OLYMPIC **.65**
Specially baked delicious Grecian loaf filled with layers of tenderly grilled ham and melted cheese, lettuce, tomato and sauce.

CHEESEBURGER, Tender big hamburger, blanketed with melted, mellow cheese on
  a toasted bun .... .35
DELUXE CHEESEBURGER, Delicious cheeseburger glorified with lettuce, tomato and
  our sauce .... .40
GRILLED CHEESE, Three slices of fine American cheese grilled on fresh white bread,
  pickle chips .... .30
HAM, Grilled or baked, tender, choice sugar cured ham slice — hot or cold with
  lettuce and mayonnaise .... .50
GRILLED HAM & CHEESE, Enjoy together the flavor of hot ham smothered with rich
  American cheese .... .60
BREADED PORK CUTLET, Tender Cutlet with tangy barbecue sauce .... .55

All sandwiches on crisp toasted bun (or bread) with your choice of lettuce, jumbo sauce, mayonnaise, pickle, relish, mustard, catsup or onion

SOUPS, SALADS AND TASTE TREATS

CHILI, Made with lean beef, choice chili beans and the right seasonings .... .35
NAVY BEAN SOUP, Rich and wholesome. We make it .... .25
COTTAGE CHEESE & FRUIT, Large order of dairy fresh cottage cheese and fruit,
  served with crackers .... .75
CHEF'S SALAD BOWL, Luncheon delight with crisp lettuce, tomatoes and hard boiled
  eggs, hot fresh baked roll .... .85
  Choice of French, Thousand Island, Vinegar & Oil, Mayonnaise and Bleu Cheese Dressing
  A LA CARTE: Chef's Salad, Head Lettuce .... .25   Chicken .... .90
               Cole Slaw, Fruit Gelatin, Apple Sauce .20   Pieces of Fish ...... .25

A 1962 menu from the Parkmoor shows how similar its menu items were to Frisch's.
Courtesy of the Public Library of Cincinnati and Hamilton County.

particular location on Friday nights, there were dances in the parking lots with live bands.

Still another burger concept, Sandy's, had two locations in Cincinnati: one in Mount Washington on Beechmont, known as #27, and one on Glenway

Hey fans! Hear all **U.C.**
BASKETBALL GAMES
at home and away, 1961-62 season **WCPO** AM FM
brought to you by **CARTER'S** Restaurants

... where the Big Burger chef creates the original
BIG BURGER

... and exclusively at Carter's
COLONEL SANDERS' RECIPE
Kentucky Fried Chicken

Close to Home ... Close as Your Phone

- ROSELAWN
7635 Reading Rd.—PO 1-3242
- NEWPORT
SHOPPING CENTER
CO 1-3332

- WESTERN HILLS
SHOPPING CENTER
6020 Glenway—MO 1-7070
- BRENTWOOD
8590 Winton Rd.—JA 2-2535

- MONTGOMERY
9300 Montgomery Rd.—SY 1-9366
- MONFORT HEIGHTS
North Bend & Cheviot Rds. MO 2-3322

- EVENDALE
9972 Reading Rd.—PR 1-33
- Hamilton, Oh
3010 Dixie Highway

A 1960s Carter's ad shows that it served Kentucky Fried Chicken. *Courtesy of the University of Cincinnati Library.*

Avenue at the corner of Muddy Creek, known as #28. They were formed by four McDonald's franchisees who felt they were swindled out of their California franchises by Ray Kroc. Using a mascot of a dark-haired girl with a Scottish kilted hat, Sandy's was a play on the name McDonald's; it was in litigation with McDonald's until settling out of court in the 1960s.

Mike Naseef, an Illinios native, heard that Sandy's was opening two stores in Cincinnati. His good friend Gene Wymer was to manage the Beechmont store, and Wymer got him the gig at the Westside store. So, Naseef moved his wife and two sons to Cincinnati and, after training two weeks in a Moline, Illinois store, operated the most profitable Sandy's in the entire chain.

Sandy's was known for its BigScots burger, HiLo double-decker, French fries, onion rings and shakes. Naseef's location became popular as a cruise-up spot for West High and Oak Hills high school teenagers. It ran promos like free hamburgers on St. Paddy's Day if you dyed your hair green, raffled off a turkey at Thanksgiving and had a raffle to see ice skater Dorothy Hamill when she came to town.

When the fish sandwich came to the Sandy's menu around the same time as the McDonald's fish sandwich invented by Groen, the Glenway location was the third to get it. Sandy's executives originally didn't want it because it deviated from the menu. Naseef said that he would sell 1,500 to 2,000 fish sandwiches per hour at Glenway because the population was 80 percent Catholic. It became popular with school kids from Our Lady of Lourdes, down the street, who would come during their lunch hour. Eventually the school stopped the kids from leaving at lunch because it was affecting business at the school cafeteria!

Naseef kept the chain after the 1973 merger with Hardee's and operated independently until 1982, taking off the *S* from his sign to avoid copyright infringement. Its signature double-decker burger, the Hi-Lo, is so popular that a group re-creates it every year at the West Side Street Festival. Made using butternut burger buns, Tone's onions and American cheese slices, people come from all over Cincinnati to taste this nostalgic burger.

Another local fast-food chain that had locations around Cincinnati before McDonald's predominated was the Red Barn. Founded in 1961 in Springfield, Ohio, by Don Six, Martin Levine and Jim Kirsch, the locations were purchased in 1963 and moved briefly to Dayton, Ohio. Then, in the late 1970s, Servomation bought the company, which was in turn bought by Motel 6 in the late 1970s. Only interested in Servomation, Motel 6 stopped advertising for the chain and allowed the franchisee leases to expire. In Cincinnati, there were locations in North College Hill at 6715 Hamilton Avenue, Vine Street in Over-the-Rhine, Reading at Lincoln, 8259 Colerain Avenue, 7131 Reading Road and 3604 Harrison Avenue.

Known for its distinct barn building, its menu was ahead of its time. The Big Barney, its two-patty burger, predated the Big Mac by a few years. It also had a burger called the Barnbuster that was similar to a Quarter Pounder or Whopper. Also known for its fried chicken, Red Barn was the first chain to have self-service salad bars, a trend that took off in the 1970s. Chicken and fish were fried in pure vegetable oil and fries and onion rings in a 60 percent vegetable oil/40 percent lard mix for extra flavor.

Before the fish chains like Arthur Treacher's and Long John Silver's came to town, a Cincinnati couple, Hal and Chris Wehling, started a popular fish and chips concept called Squire Jacks in 1969. Their first store was on Eire Avenue in Hyde Park. Remembering the delicious fish and chips places that he frequented during his school days in London, England, Hal looked at the success of Kentucky Fried Chicken, thinking that he could do the same thing with fish and chips. They used to wrap theirs in faux-newspaper wax paper. There were stores in Silverton, Roselawn, Hartwell and surrounding areas, a total of seven. Staying close

An ad for Red Barn shows two West High girls enjoying a quick snack after school. *Courtesy of Price Hill Historical Society.*

to their fish supply chain, in the middle of 1970 they made it through a fish shortage by stockpiling quality frozen fish in a warehouse, while some of their chain competitors were forced to close stores. Arthur Treacher's, based out of Columbus, Ohio, was no competition, but when Long John Silver's came to Cincinnati, it pushed Squire Jacks out of business.

Becoming a Big Boy

Frisch's won the battle of all the Cincinnati drive-in restaurants. Samuel Frisch, the founding father, opened the Frisch Café on Freeman Avenue downtown in 1905. In 1910, he sold the Freeman café, moving his family to the growing village of Norwood. There he opened a restaurant at 4664 Montgomery Road. After success with the first café, in 1915 he opened Frisch's Stag Lunch in a new building, joined by his sons Dave, Irving and Reuben. After his death in 1923, twenty-year-old Dave managed the restaurant. Dave sold out to his brothers in 1932, opening two other Frisch's cafés. Although Frisch's Café was successful, the effects of the Depression led to bankruptcy, and both cafés closed in 1938.

Dave soon found Fred Cornuelle, a local entrepreneur and investor. With Cornuelle's funding, David Frisch opened his Mainliner in 1939 on Wooster Pike in Fairfax, named after a passenger plane that flew into nearby Lunken Airport. As Cincinnati's first year-round drive-in, it became successful. A second restaurant was opened in 1944, constructed to resemble Washington's Mount Vernon home.

Around the time of World War II, Dave Frisch visited one of Bob Wian's Big Boy restaurants in California. Although not able to meet Wian, Frisch was impressed by the double-patty Big Boy hamburger and saw the efficiency of two thinner beef patties cooking faster than a single thicker patty.

Wian, meanwhile, was dealing with drive-in operators outside California riding on his brand's coattails and using the Big Boy name without his permission. Wian needed his Big Boy restaurants to operate outside California to maintain national trademark protection. When they finally met, Wian offered Frisch a deal of one dollar per year for a territory including Ohio, Kentucky, Indiana and Florida. Frisch accepted and became the first Big Boy franchisee. Dave Frisch began selling Big Boy hamburgers in 1946 at his Frisch's Mainliner Drive-In. The first Frisch's Big Boy Drive-In restaurant, "Big Boy One," opened in 1948 on Central Parkway north of downtown Cincinnati.

An early carhop Frisch's location on the Westside shows its popularity with high schoolers. *Courtesy of the Price Hill Historical Society.*

Frisch's ... *nationally famous features of the house*

BIG BOY Two Patties of Ground Beef, Melted Cheese, Pickle, Shredded Lettuce, Topped Off with Our Own Frisch Sauce .... .55
BIG BOY PLATTER French Fries, Cole Slaw .... .90

BRAWNY LAD Big, Tender Chopped Choice Steak on Toasted Rye Bun with a Slice of Bermuda Onion .... .55
Brawny Lad Platter, French Fries, Cole Slaw .... .90

BONELESS FILET OF SOLE SANDWICH
on Toasted Bun, with Lettuce and Tartar Sauce .... .65
Filet of Sole Platter French Fries, Cole Slaw 1.00
By the Piece to Go .... .35

BUDDIE BOY Grilled Ham and Swiss Cheese, Tomato, Shredded Lettuce, Frisch Sauce on a Special French Roll ... .65

CHOPPED PORK TENDERLOIN SANDWICH
with Tomato Slice and Frisch Sauce on a Toasted Bun .... .60

Sandwiches

REGULAR HAMBURGER .... .30
  with Lettuce and Frisch Sauce
DE LUXE—Plus Onion and Tomato 40
REGULAR CHEESEBURGER ..... .35
  with Lettuce and Frisch Sauce
DE LUXE—Plus Onion and Tomato 45
GRILLED AMERICAN CHEESE .... .30
  in Butter
COLD HAM SANDWICH .... .60
  with Lettuce and Mayonnaise
HAM & CHEESE COMBINATION .. .70
  with Lettuce and Mayonnaise
BACON-TOMATO COMBINATION 60
  with Lettuce and Mayonnaise
EGG SALAD SANDWICH .... .30
  on Homemade Bread, Toasted
AMERICAN OR SWISS CHEESE ... .30
  with Lettuce and Mayonnaise
CHICKEN SNACK ON TOAST .... .85
  One-Quarter of Finest Quality Chicken
  with French Fries
SMALL FILET OF SOLE .... .40
  on Toasted Bun with Lettuce, Tartar Sauce

Pancakes

Old Fashioned Golden Brown
Pancakes Served with Plenty of
Butter, Maple Syrup .... .40
Pancakes with
  Ham (4 oz.) .... .95
  Bacon (3 Strips) .... .80
  Sausage (2 Patties) .... .80

Low Calorie Plate
Tender Beef Patty with

Soups-Chili
We Make Our Own From a Recipe Handed Down From Generation to Generation

CHILI WITH BEANS .... .40
VEGETABLE SOUP .... .25
CLAM CHOWDER ...... .25
SOUP OF THE DAY ...... .25
CHILI AND SPAGHETTI ... .60

Salads

Hearts of Lettuce .... ,
  (Choice of French, Bleu Cheese,
  1,000 Island, Caesar or
  Green Goddess Dressing)
Sliced Tomatoes ....
  Choice of Dressing
Cole Slaw ....

Chef's Salad Bowl, Tomato Wedges,
  Julienne Ham and Cheese ...... .75
Tossed Salad .... .30
  Choice of Dressing
Cottage Cheese 30; with Pineapple 50
  With Tomato .... .45

Appetizers

Chilled Tomato Juice 15-30
Chilled Orange Juice 15-30
Chilled Grapefruit Juice 15-30

Onion Rings

A 1949 menu from Frisch's Big Boy in Cincinnati. *Courtesy of the Public Library of Cincinnati and Hamilton County.*

Being the first franchisee, Dave Frisch was allowed some unique freedoms. Wian dressed his Big Boy hamburgers with thousand island dressing, but Frisch eventually changed this to his own homemade tartar sauce and used dill pickles. This made Frisch's Big Boy unique from most other Big Boy restaurants. Frisch's tartar sauce became the signature sauce served with other menu items and was eventually sold in jars for take-home use. Frisch recognized the efficiency of using a single condiment across the menu, and Wian adopted the same concept with his thousand island sauce. Frisch's tartar sauce became so popular in Greater Cincinnati that it was offered in 1960 to local retail grocers for sale.

Frisch's created the Brawny Lad and Swiss Miss sandwiches, which were added to the menus of most other Big Boy franchisees. The chopped sirloin sandwiches are both served on rye buns.

In 1983, Frisch's reinvented itself by adding drive-thru service. It also introduced the soup and salad bar, jumping on the new trend in fast food. These new concepts made remodeling or demo-and-rebuilding older restaurants necessary to stay competitive. Today, Frisch's remains an iconic restaurant brand in Cincinnati.

THE HITCHING POST RESTAURANTS

The Hitching Post was a Cincinnati fried chicken chain that started on the Westside and was known for its "World's Best Fried Chicken." James G. Kent opened the first restaurant at 5259 Glenway Avenue in 1955. While the chain is now defunct, two former chain locations still operate today as independent restaurants with the same name. The Hitching Post preceded KFC and differed from other chicken places in that it was a sit-down family restaurant with a full-service menu. It was not a drive-up like Carter's, which served KFC-brand fried chicken and had locations on Montgomery Road and Springfield Pike, or the Parkmoor, which served Dixie-brand golden fried chicken at downtown, Roselawn and Peebles' Corner locations.

Kent opened a second location in 1957 at Warsaw Avenue in Price Hill that only lasted a year, and then he had Earl Carlson manage a location at Woodford Road in Pleasant Ridge in 1959. By 1962, Reading Road in Reading, Colerain Avenue in Groesbeck and Harrison Avenue in Bridgetown locations had been added to the original Glenway Avenue and Pleasant Ridge locations. Soon Ludlow Avenue in Clifton, North Bend Road in Cheviot and Delhi Pike in Delhi Hills locations were added. The Cheviot chain was owned by James's brother, Alex, and his wife, Beatrice. The Hyde Park location followed in the early 1960s, the Kellogg Avenue location in 1968 and, finally, a Greenhills Shopping Center location.

When the franchise folded, the Bridgetown location, owned by Ron Larkin, became Ron's Roost, and the Clifton location became the Proud Rooster, which is not associated with the Westside restaurant by the same name. Honoring the family diner feel of the Hitching Post, both restaurants remain successful with home-style menus.

The Hyde Park location on Madison Avenue was purchased by brother-and-sister duo Frank and Peggy Kahsar in the 1980s. They still use the original recipe for hand-breaded fresh chicken, fried to order. Also famous for their kettle cakes, which are a crescent-shaped version of beignets, they serve up breakfast and other home-style dishes like liver and onions to loyal and new customers alike.

The Kellogg Avenue location, another independent, family-owned spot, has a 1960s roadside diner feel. You will see the original flashing-bulb sign with the smiling black horse logo and see how an original freestanding restaurant looked. If you like extra-crispy chicken, you will like it here, fried in lard and orderable up to one hundred pieces for large gatherings. Its menu also includes its special recipe of Cincinnati-style chili, fried gizzards, fish sandwiches, goetta, whole pies and homemade salads like potato, macaroni and coleslaw.

The 1970s and 1980s saw the smorgasbord trend come to Cincinnati—names like Duff's on Reading Road, David's Buffet on Reading Road in Evendale and on Ohio Pike in Western Hills, Schueller's on Glenway in Price Hill, Old Farm

The original 1960s Hitching Post sign at the Kellogg Avenue location, claiming the "World's Best Fried Chicken." *Author's collection.*

A Schueler's Smorgasbord advertisement that markets one of the many that popped up in Cincinnati in the 1970s. *Courtesy of Price Hill Historical Society.*

Smorgasteria on Reading Road and Homer's Original Smorgasbord on Reading Road in Sharonville.

Homer Duff owned an IGA grocery store in Lebanon, Ohio, in the 1970s that became the birthplace of a nationwide chain of buffet-style restaurants. He noticed that meat cut too early would have to be discarded at the end of the day. Although it was still good, it was discolored, and people would not buy it.

Duff decided to use the leftover meat at a sandwich bar at the corner of the supermarket. It cost ninety-nine cents for a meal. This concept grew, and soon Duff was selling the supermarket to open a real restaurant with the "one meal for one price" buffet concept. He also came up with an unusual concept branded "Circl-Serv," for the buffet circling around the customer rather than the opposite, and patented the idea. The circling buffet entered the kitchen, where workers would refill empty bins before it circled back. It circled thirty pans at the rate of one revolution every three minutes and could serve 450 patrons per hour, about double that of a straight-line buffet, and was constantly being restocked.

Duff sold the entire successful business in 1983 to Kelly Johnson, and the restaurants peaked at 150 locations across the country. Johnson filed for bankruptcy, and Granada Inc. took over in 1989 but soon lost interest in the Duff concept; the majority of locations began to close.

Chapter 5

DOWNTOWN RESTAURANTS

Cincinnati's fine dining was originally found at downtown hotels and taverns. Here in the "West," bed and board pretty much went together well into the nineteenth century. As we evolved, Cincinnati's fine dining moved out of the hotels and into other prime downtown locations.

THE MAISONETTE AND LA NORMANDIE

The Maisonette is Cincinnati's icon of fine dining. Open for fifty-six years, the restaurant carried the *Mobil Travel Guide* five-star rating for forty-one consecutive years, starting in 1964. Founded by Russian immigrant Nathan Comisar in 1949 at Walnut Street in the Fountain Square Building, it was named for the nightspot in New York City's St. Regis Hotel where he courted his wife, Vallie. Originally serving spaghetti and meatballs, it didn't transform into the famous French restaurant until its first chef, Maurice Gorodesky, was hired in 1953.

Nat ran several restaurants in Cincinnati in the 1920s, including his deli. Twenty years later, the Comisar food empire included restaurants like the Pirate Den, Comisar's Grill, Paradise Garden and La Normandie, which opened in 1931. Sadly, Nat died shortly after his dream restaurant, the Maisonette, opened, but Vallie and their son Lee stepped in and ran the restaurant until brother Michael J. permanently came aboard in the early 1960s.

FAVORITE RECIPES OF EMIL YOST
Hotel Sinton, St. Nicholas, Cincinnati, Ohio

BEEF POT ROAST A LA MODE

4 lbs. beef shoulder, chuck or rump
1 quart cider or red wine
3 cloves
1 bay leaf
2 tablespoons American Beauty Open Kettle Rendered Lard
2 carrots
2 onions
2 tablespoons flour
½ cup canned or fresh tomatoes

Salt and pepper the beef, add cloves, bay leaf, cider or wine and let marinate 5 or 6 hours. Remove meat and wipe with a cloth. Brown meat, carrots and onions in a pan with the lard. Add flour and brown. Then add 1 cup marinate and the tomatoes, cover meat with stock or water, season and simmer until done. Remove fat before serving and use noodles as garnish.

FAVORITE RECIPES OF CLOVIS CHARTRON
Chef, Netherland Plaza Hotel, Cincinnati, Ohio

BOILED BEEF—NETHERLAND PLAZA

4 lbs. Fresh Beef Brisket, Parboil 15 minutes. Place in deep casserole. Cover with fresh water and boil 2 to 2½ hours. 1 hour before meat is cooked, add carrots, onions, leeks and small head of cabbage. Add potatoes before cooked. Remove meat and place on platter with vegetables around. Serve with horseradish sauce.

HORSERADISH SAUCE: 1 glass horseradish (grated). Squeeze out all vinegar thoroughly. 1 cup of broth from the beef. Put broth in pan, add horseradish and a small lump of butter (about ½ the size of an egg). Add 1 full teaspoon sugar and let contents come to a boil. Mix in about ¼ cup white bread crumbs and stir until all is well creamed. This will serve 8 people.

Above: The 1930s downtown hotel chefs Emil Yost from the St. Nicholas and Clovis Chartron from Netherland Plaza were as celebrated as today's downtown chefs. *Author's collection.*

Left: A portrait of Nathan Comisar, the founder of the Maisonette in Cincinnati. *Courtesy of the Public Library of Cincinnati and Hamilton County.*

Lee and Michael Comisar acquired the iconic building on Sixth Street with black awnings and black iron balconies in 1966, two years after their mother passed. The atmosphere was high formal, but it was not based on East Coast glitz or West Coast glamour—rather, just solid service, a Midwest work ethic and standout French dishes. The most popular tables were nos. 50 and 51, front and center, with high visibility.

The Comisars would branch out with other food ventures like Bistro Gigi in Mariemont; Newport Beach in Newport, Kentucky; Chester's Roadhouse on Montgomery; and even a stint at ownership of the historic Golden Lamb, in Lebanon, Ohio.

Maisonette employed five chefs de cuisine in its history. Maurice Gorodesky (1953–56) was the first and served the shortest tenure. Chef Gorodesky left Maisonette in 1956 to start Pigall's restaurant at Fifth and Pike Street downtown, named after a former red-light district in Paris. Pierre Adrien (1956–72) was next, the first of three chefs to obtain the

A photo of the original location of the Maisonette on Walnut Street. *Courtesy of Michael Comisar.*

five-star rating. Georges Haiden (1972–93), known for his classic French cuisine, came next. One of the favorite dishes under Haiden's regime was the Raspberry Chicken. Jean Robert de Cavel (1993–2001), with his signature "Mad Hatter" hair, came next. He would become known for his Nouveau French cuisine with an American twist. Cavel was the one out of all the Maisonette chefs who created the most impact on the Cincinnati food scene. Chef Cavel mentored chefs who left and started their own restaurants. One such chef, David Falk, would go on to open the very popular Boca and Nada restaurants. Another chef who worked under Cavel, Nate Appleman, went on to head Chipotle's menu development. Cavel promised three to five years at Maisonette but stayed seven and has been in Cincinnati ever since, opening restaurants like Jean Robert at Pigall's (2002–9), JeanRo Bistro, Pho Paris (2004–8), Table (2010), French Crust (2013) and La Bar a Boeuf (2015) in the up-and-coming East Walnut Hills neighborhood.

One of the most important restaurants Cavel partnered to open, with the Wade family, was Lavomatic, named after a French laundry, which was an urban beachhead to what would become the Gateway Corridor Entertainment District in the re-gentrified Over-the-Rhine. When Chef Cavel left Maisonette in 2001 to reopen Pigall's, Chef Bertrand Bouquin, from Nevers in southern Burgundy, France, took over until Maisonette's close on July 25, 2005.

It was a change of the food scene in Cincinnati that ultimately led to the demise of the Maisonette. It became a place where people only went on special occasions, aside from the small but wealthy clientele that came into town from the suburbs on a weekly basis. And the modern economy squeezed out the expensive business lunches that also supported fine dining. The suit coat atmosphere became a thing of the past, and Cincinnatians searched for quality and value, not formality. Chef Cavel said of the Cincinnati food scene when he arrived in 1993, "Cincinnati had fine dining and very casual, and nothing in between. The gap is filled with many more that are chef-driven and supporting local products." Cavel filled this gap himself with his restaurant ventures, and he legitimized the redevelopment of Over-the-Rhine into the foodie mecca it is today. Cavel was raised in a river town in northern France, Lille, in a close-knit Catholic family, so Cincinnati, with all the support that its omnivores have given him, feels very much like home.

The Comisars would blame the demise of their clientele on the Cincinnati Riots of 2001, the 9/11 tragedy and the flailing economy. But during the same time, the new Aronoff Center for the Arts and its Backstage District was burgeoning right at Maisonette's doorstep. The fact was that Maisonette knew the changes it needed to make to stay on trend, but it was not able to make them in time to save itself.

After a threat to move if the city didn't give Maisonette $4 million, Mayor Charlie Luken called the Comisar family's bluff and wished them well in their move to the surburbs or across the river to northern Kentucky. Both moves fell through, and Maisonette is now in the annals of Cincinnati food history.

Nat polled the former staff on their favorite celebrity visitors over the years. Although he didn't get a concise answer, he did get a huge list of celebrities who enjoyed the Maisonette: Frank Sinatra, Michael Douglas, William Shatner, Richard Dreyfuss, Liberace, Bobby Flay, Michael Stipe, Jimmy Buffett, Sharon Stone, Suzanne Somers, Sammy Davis Jr., Rob Lowe and many others.

In the last few years at Maisonette, popular items were the crab bisque; the Cocktail Maisonette, consisting of champagne and framboise; Hawaiian snapper cerviche; and the most requested dessert, the white chocolate mousse. Today, those who want recipes from the old Maisonette can opt-in to Nat Comisar's Sibcy Cline realty newsletter, from which he sent over recipes from the old icon, including the following.

Shrimp Maisonette

1 soup spoon of fresh chopped parsley
2 ounces fresh shallots, chopped
1 teaspoon fresh garlic, chopped
4 ounces sweet butter, softened
salt and pepper
3 ounces dry white wine
12 large shrimp, peeled and deveined
16 mushroom caps, sliced

Combine the parsley, shallots, garlic and butter. Mix well. Add salt and pepper. Melt the mixture in a heavy skillet. Add the wine and bring to a boil. Add the shrimp and mushrooms. Lower heat and cook lightly. Spoon out the shrimp and the mushroom on plates. Reduce the cooking liquid, adjust seasoning and pour onto shrimp and mushrooms. Serve with toast.

Chef David Falk's third incarnation of Boca took over the former Maisonette space in 2013, and Sotto, Falk's Italian Trattoria, would take over the former La Normandie space.

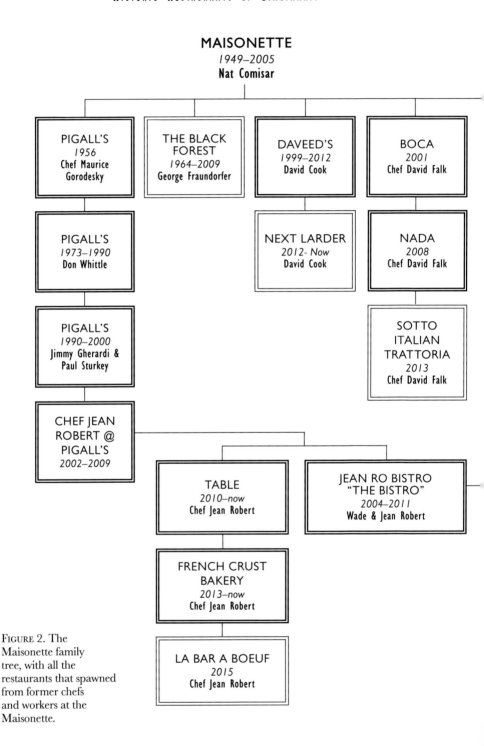

FIGURE 2. The Maisonette family tree, with all the restaurants that spawned from former chefs and workers at the Maisonette.

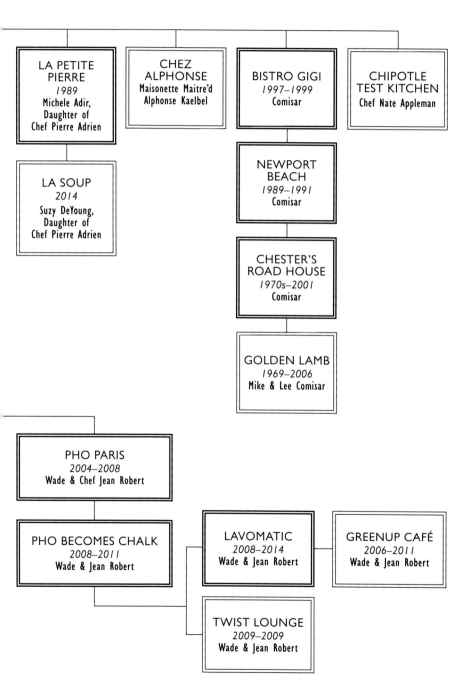

LA PETITE PIERRE
1989
Michele Adir,
Daughter of
Chef Pierre Adrien

CHEZ ALPHONSE
Maisonette Maitre'd
Alphonse Kaelbel

BISTRO GIGI
1997–1999
Comisar

CHIPOTLE TEST KITCHEN
Chef Nate Appleman

LA SOUP
2014
Suzy DeYoung,
Daughter of
Chef Pierre Adrien

NEWPORT BEACH
1989–1991
Comisar

CHESTER'S ROAD HOUSE
1970s–2001
Comisar

GOLDEN LAMB
1969–2006
Mike & Lee Comisar

PHO PARIS
2004–2008
Wade & Chef Jean Robert

PHO BECOMES CHALK
2008–2011
Wade & Jean Robert

LAVOMATIC
2008–2014
Wade & Jean Robert

GREENUP CAFÉ
2006–2011
Wade & Jean Robert

TWIST LOUNGE
2009–2009
Wade & Jean Robert

From 1970 to 1973, Cincinnati was called a "gastronomical Camelot," but only if by Camelot you really meant Paris, Burgundy or Provence. Cincinnati had the unique fortune of three Mobil-rated five-star French restaurants: the Maisonette, the Gourmet Room at the Terrace Park Hilton and Pigall's. Even though all were French restaurants, the three were slightly different. Pigall's was more French Provincial cuisine, the Gourmet Room was Parisian style and Maisonette was haute cuisine. Foodies would fly into Cincinnati from New York or Chicago and go to Maisonette for dinner, the Gourmet Room the next night and then Pigall's the night after that.

Gourmet Restaurant

Also known as the Gourmet Room, this exclusive twenty-table restaurant debuted in 1948 and occupied what looked like a spaceship that landed on the twentieth-floor rooftop of the Terrace Plaza Hotel. Following the mid-century modern aesthetic of the hotel, the Spanish surrealist Joan Miró's dramatic thirty-foot mural graced the back wall behind the curved banquet. The Terrace Park Hotel was a modernist dream unlike any hotel in the United States.

Famous for its Parisian-style French cuisine, the first chef was Vito Lacaputo, an Italian trained in France. George Pulver was a Swiss-born chef in the 1980s, also French trained. Henri Gugliemi was the well-loved maitre'd for twenty years. John Kinsella and Hans Panchup were other chefs de cuisine, and George Coorey was the pianist there for forty years. In addition to achieving the famed five-star Michelin rating in the 1970s, the restaurant won more than ten dining awards over the years from *Holiday* magazine.

After the Emery family sold the hotel to the Hilton chain in 1965, Hilton added a bit of Parisan flamboyance to the mid-century décor with a six-foot-diameter golden bronze chandelier that had hung in the Army and Navy Club of London as a gift from Queen Victoria, gilded Regency-period wall sconces from a chateau in southern France and an eighteenth-century terra-cotta bust of Marie Antoinette from the Palace at Versailles in Paris. One very Parisian 1962 entrée item was Veal Sweatbreads on Casserole Financier with Saffron Rice for only $3.30. The restaurant closed in 1992 and now awaits a developer who can reinvent the restaurant and hotel below it.

A 1950s Gourmet Room menu cover showing a piece of the Joan Miró mural commissioned for the restaurant. *Courtesy of Public Library of Cincinnati and Hamilton County.*

Gourmet Room Chocolate Marquise

28 ounces chocolate
2 pints heavy cream
2 ounces powdered sugar
2 ounces regular sugar
½ pint Grand Marnier
12 egg yolks

Melt chocolate in double boiler. Whisk together the heavy cream and powdered sugar to make whipped cream. In a pan, add the regular sugar and Grand Marnier to the egg yolks and make an emulsion over low heat. Add to chocolate.

Whip the egg emulsion and chocolate together until you have a smooth paste. Add the whipped cream and repeat. Pour everything into a mold with parchment paper at bottom. Chill two hours, remove and serve.

The Tony Soprano of Cincinnati Steakhouses

If Nat Comisar was the marquis of French cuisine in Cincinnati, then Jeff Ruby is the godfather of steakhouses in Cincinnati. Zagat rates his steakhouses higher than any in New York City or Chicago, considered America's quintessential steak cities. Although each of Jeff Ruby's six eateries in three states is different in atmosphere, the grade of meat is the same in all restaurants. You can pass his most successful restaurant, Ruby's Steakhouse on Seventh and Walnut, and see the steaks aging in the window.

Ruby came to Cincinnati in 1970 from the Jersey Shore, where he grew up working at his mother and stepfather's restaurants. His first job here was managing the downtown Holiday Inn at Eighth and Linn Streets. In true Ruby bravado, he turned the twelfth-floor bar into the "Den of the Little Foxes" at Lucy in the Sky disco, directly competing with Hugh Heffner's Cincinnati Playboy Club. It wasn't long before he was managing all seven of the Holiday Inns in Cincinnati.

It was that confidence, along with business philosophy and instincts, that led his first investors—Reds baseball stars Pete Rose and Johnny Bench—to invest with him in his first restaurant, the Precinct, in 1981. Nobody believed it when word leaked that he was opening a high-end steakhouse in then rundown Columbia Tusculum. The old police station had fifty-two liens against the building, and the dining room only had sixty-eight seats.

But the Precinct was packed every night. The average Joe couldn't get a reservation. Athletes, eye candy and celebrities were everywhere. A disco upstairs beckoned for after dinner, and no desserts or after-dinner drinks were served to turn tables. No lunch was served. But Ruby doubled his first-year projections, and the rest is history. The Waterfront floating restaurant with Las Brisas nightclub came next in 1986; his signature Jeff Ruby Steakhouse, with an Art Deco– and Tamara de Lempicka–inspired interior, came along in 1999; Carlo and Johnny's arrived in 2001; and a Jeff Ruby Steakhouse at Belterra Casino came in 2004 and in Louisville, Kentucky, in 2006.

He's had four restaurants close in his career: Tropicana (2002–8); the Waterfont (1986–2011); his Jeff Ruby's Steakhouse (2009–10) in St. Louis, Missouri; and his venture with Bootsy Collins (2008–10).

Caproni's

In 1886, Enrico "Cap" Caproni, a fiery Tuscan immigrant, opened a new restaurant with all his savings. In a cellar room just off a narrow alley, Caproni, with his handsome moustache and kindly glow in his eyes, worked over steaming kettles on a great wood-fired stove.

His first customers were pressmen from the nearby newspaper. Before he could ask what they thought of the food, the whistle blew, and all the men rushed back to work. The next day he had his answer when all his original customers returned and brought others with them. Word spread, and soon Caproni's became the favorite eating place downtown of the well-to-do and the working people alike. All came to sample the pasta and returned for more.

As years passed, Cap expanded the restaurant and finally moved to another location at 610 Main Street, bringing the fabulous "Gaby" to preside over his kitchen. Gabriele Di Motolo was Italian born and trained to have a fine reverence for good food. After Caproni died in the early 1930s, Gaby took on the mantle and, with a host of other famous artists in Italian cuisine, continued the great feeling of warmth Cap had for the place.

In 1946, Sicilian immigrants Antonio and Carmella Palazzolo bought and managed Caproni's, making famous their osso bucco and hearty Italian

The intimate setting of the interior of Caproni's in the 1920s. *Courtesy of the Public Library of Cincinnati and Hamilton County.*

soups. Antonio had formed with his sons the Antonio Palazzolo Company, a wholesale Italian grocery and import business. The Palazzolos owned the restaurant until 1965, but their Italian food legacy didn't end there. Antonio Sr.'s grandson, also Antonio, opened Antonio's of Hyde Park, after his father Dominic and Uncle Pete developed Hyde Park Plaza in 1985.

Hailed as one of the finest Italian restaurants in the nation, as well as the oldest in the city, Caproni's continued to provide its customers with authentic Italian cuisine in pleasant surroundings for eighty-nine years until it closed in 1975. It achieved the admirable position of being one of the few restaurants in Cincinnati to have a billboard in the outfield wall of Crosley Field.

SCOTTI'S

Scotti's restaurant on 919 Vine Street, at 103 years old, is the longest-running family-owned restaurant in the city. If you're a multigenerational Cincinnatian, it's a restaurant where your great-grandparents could have courted. Its red-and-green 1930s neon sign beckons patrons into its two-story façade. It resembles the type of narrow old building you might find in the winding streets of any Italian town. Inside you will find walls decked with a mosaic of mismatched and broken tiles and tables decked out in the standard red-and-white checked tablecloths, with old chianti bottles being used as candleholders. It's like a scene out of a 1950s Federico Fellini movie, like *La Dolce Vita*. Was it the *Genius des Wassers* on Fountain Square you just came from or the Trevi fountain? The dark, windowless interior and Italian opera music might make you forget.

The restaurant has been owned and run by the same Italian immigrant family since its founding in 1912. Calabrian native Salvatore Scoleri, the founder, had just moved to Cincinnati from Philadelphia. He and his wife, Concetta, had been operating the European Hotel in Philadelphia with Concetta's mother, Teresa Saltera. For some reason, Salvatore had to leave Philadelphia, a reason the family still knows nothing about—or at least no one's talking. Salvatore named the restaurant after his friend Antonio Scotti, a famous Metropolitan Opera singer. It's no surprise that only Italian opera music is played inside. The current owners are the great-grandchildren of Salvatore Scoleri: Marco DiMarco, Tenerina (Rina) DiMarco Searles and Pasquale (Pat) DiMarco. On occasion, you may also find the great-great-grandchildren of Scoleri working at the restaurant.

The exterior of Scotti's restaurant on Vine Street, showing its one-hundred-year anniversary banner. *Author's collection.*

The owners say their restaurant is like "visiting the Italian grandmother you never had."

Guido DiMarco was the third owner before handing it over to his kids. His aunt, Amelia Scoleri, used to make all the noodles by hand. Guido's mother, Tenerina "Teddi" Scoleri DiMarco (Salvatore's daughter), demanded certain behaviors and were known to throw patrons out if they didn't abide. She scolded many a customer who wasn't able to eat their gargantuan portions.

Scotti's is not all about spaghetti and meatballs, although a side of spaghetti and red sauce comes with every entrée. The menu has about every Italian pasta dish you can imagine, including favorites like ravioli, fettucini and lasagna, as well as a half page of different types of veal scaloppini, the Italian schnitzel. The DiMarcos use the same five-generation-old recipes from Concetta Scoleria and her mother, Teresa, from Calabria, the southern tip of Italy across from Sicily, where deep-red tomato sauce and lots of garlic emanate the cuisine.

Scotti's Scallopini ala Marsala con Fungi

¼ pound butter
1¼ pounds veal, cut in thin slices
flour
Marsala wine
5 mushrooms, sliced thin
salt
white pepper
parsley, chopped

Melt one stick of butter in a 12-inch skillet over low heat. Dredge the veal in flour. Place floured veal in the hot melted butter. Saute 2 minutes on each side. Pour one cup of Marsala wine over the veal. Add mushrooms, salt and pepper. Cover and simmer 5 minutes. Remove the veal from skillet and plate. Top with mushrooms. Sprinkle top with parsley.

CINCINNATI'S FIRST CHINESE FOOD

Chinese food had made it to Cincinnati by 1900, about a half a century later than its introduction in the United States in San Francisco's Chinese immigrant community. A 1920 report claimed that Cincinnati had only 20 members in its Chinese immigrant community, all from the province of Canton. Compared to other cities of similar size, Cincinnati's community lagged in its population. Dayton's Chinese community, for example, numbered over 150 in 1920.

Cincinnati's chop suey houses catered to the lower and working classes and were often in less than respectable areas of the city. In 1907, the *Cincinnati Post* estimated that there were about ten chop suey houses in Cincinnati. In 1912, the *Cincinnati Enquirer* reported that a number of Cincinnati's Chinese restaurants were serving alcohol illegally. Sam Lee, the proprietor of a chop suey house at Carlisle Avenue and John Street, was one of those accused.

Canton, from which all of Cincinnati's Chinese immigrants hailed, was also where the revolution against the Qing dynasty had led up to the creation of the Republic of China in 1912. The last days of the Qing dynasty in the late nineteenth century were marked by civil unrest and foreign invasions and were the reason many immigrated to America for a better life. For those entrepreneurial spirits, Cincinnati offered a fertile market for new Chinese restaurants.

A report from a member of the Cincinnati Chapter of the American Electrical Workers Union reported on the state of Chinese restaurants in Cincinnati in 1922 for his fellow brothers working in the area:

> *About 15 years ago in the 200 block of West Sixth street, the second floor of a dilapidated two story building was occupied by Shanghi Lou, who conducted a Chinese Restaurant. A poorly illuminated sign over the sidewalk displayed the words "Chop Soy." Patrons here were mostly of the underworld or the occasional few whose curiosity aroused them to the point of making a visit.*
>
> *As a contrast to the above we now have at Sixth and Main [in the heart of the city] one of the most modern chop suey houses in the country. It also happens that the proprietor is the same Shanghi Lou, who employs Wong Yie, as a manager. Aroused by both curiosity and hunger, I have several times dined with Wong Yie. I have never seen this place overly crowded, but always a gradual coming and going of patrons who have little regard for regular eating hours. About 40 small tables which accommodate two couples, and perhaps a dozen for party or family uses are spotted over the spacious floor. Japanese shades decorate the light fixtures and all other decorations are either of Japanese or Chinese design, which are not extremely elaborate but very tastefully arranged.*
>
> *Upon being seated, a Chinese waiter is immediately at your service. Unless you are familiar with the bill of fare, considerable amount of time will be taken up selecting something which no doubt you will be unable to*

eat after it is served (because of utensils not food quality). Chow mein, Yoco mein, Warmein, Chicken Foo Yong or Plain Chop Suey may all appear the same on the bill of fare to one on their initial visit. But after you have been here several times, in fact often enough to call your favorite waiter by his first name, and have mastered the art of giving your order properly, you will have discovered many an appetizing dish and strenuous effort, on your part, will be required to prevent your abandoning your favorite dining place and becoming a regular with Wong Yie.

It would be Wong Yie (1875–1926) who would take chop suey and Chinese-Cantonese cuisine in Cincinnati out of the underworld and into the elite as a new "exotic" dining fare. He had come to Cincinnati by way of Harvard and started a restaurant in partnership with his cousin Wong Kee. Unlike others, he had that panache to be in the headlines and seduce the elite to patronize his restaurant.

Wong Yie was manager of a restaurant at 628 Vine called the Golden Dragon from 1900 to 1914, where he hosted Cincinnati's Chinese New Year's celebrations. Wong would also operate the Quen Lung Company, a supplier of Chinese teas, out of his residence at 121 Court Street in the 1910s. In 1912, Wong Yie threw a huge New Year's celebration at his restaurant to commemorate the birth of the Republic of China that year. In 1914, he and his wife, Lee Mon, celebrated the birth of their daughter, Wong Gut Ting, the first Chinese American born in Cincinnati. Then, in 1922, he renovated the second floor of a building at 38 East Sixth Street and Main Street, in the Washington Bank Building, into a Chinese restaurant that by 1926 had become Wong Yie's Famous Restaurant. His wife, daughters Ping and Ting and young son, Lan, would help in the operations.

Wong Yie's restaurant was large, clean and exotic, with Chinese lanterns hanging from the ceilings. He himself was very articulate in English and apparently well educated. In 1914, the *Cincinnati Commercial* asked him his thoughts on the brewing war in Europe. "Perhaps the most notable and best-cultured Chinaman in Cincinnati is Wong Yie, who conducts a restaurant at 628 Vine Street." Aside from his restaurant operations, he found time to speak in front of the Cincinnati Advertisers Club in the 1920s on the benefits of trade with China and also traveled with a Cincinnati mining group to inspect mines in Colorado.

Wong Yie's restaurant became the de facto meeting place for a number of Cincinnati society groups like the City Club, the Kiwanis Club and numerous Women's Auxiliary Organizations, as well as city politicians.

Wong Yie's restaurant at Sixth Street, with his daughter Wong Gut Ting posing for the camera. *Courtesy of the Public Library of Cincinnati and Hamilton County.*

After Wong Yie's death in 1926, his wife and children operated the restaurant into the mid-1960s, paving the way for other successful immigrant-run Chinese restaurants.

TUCKER'S

In the 1940s, the founders of Tucker's, Escom Garth "E.G" Tucker and Maynie Tucker, came up to Over-the-Rhine from Somerset, Kentucky, in the migration that took thousands to Ohio's cities looking for factory jobs after the Appalachian coal mines shut down. After finding a factory job, E.G. saw the restaurant for sale at Thirteenth Street and pleaded with Maynie to quit her job at the Baldwin Piano Company. She did, and in 1946, they opened the first iteration of Tucker's. That location had been the site of an old German tavern where the American Turner movement was founded in 1848 in this previously German working-class enclave. Tucker's diner served workers and families around the clock. Using the best ingredients the couple could find, the dishes were hearty workingman's fare. They served dishes like chicken and dumplings and chopped steak in tomato gravy. E.G. would drive around the backlots of produce vendors at Findlay Market, buying

A smiling Carla presides as queen over the grill at Tucker's Restaurant, a neighborhood staple for more than sixty years in Over-the-Rhine. *Courtesy of Tucker's Restaurant.*

produce at end-of-day discounts, and then would hit the slaughterhouses for scraps sold at pennies.

Now owned by E.G.'s son, Joe, and his wife, Carla, the exceptional menu is Carla's doing. She added meatless chili and other vegan options to please students from neighboring School for Creative and Performing Arts. And breakfast is not without goetta, made from Holtmann Meat Market's old recipe. Lunchers can try shrimp and grits or the Big Tucker Burger on the Formica counter or in a cozy booth to the side at the Vine Street location, around the corner from the original, and now in the fashionable Gateway Corridor District. It remains the friendliest little place on Vine Street.

MILLS

The Mills Cafeteria in downtown Cincinnati created an incredible atmosphere. It was the brainchild of James O. Mills, a restaurateur from Columbus, Ohio, and was a unique self-service, cafeteria type of restaurant with everyday food. Mills had grown up on a farm in Marysville, Ohio, and through his business travels saw a lack of good, wholesome, farm-fresh foods in the hotels and restaurants, like he had grown up with. He found that good food at an affordable price was a successful scheme.

Opening his first Mills cafeteria in Columbus in 1911, he opened a location in Cincinnati at 1915 near Government Square. It was the first of its kind in Cincinnati and proved an instant success, leading to the construction of a larger cafeteria that opened in 1921. The new location was dubbed "the most beautiful restaurant in America." Located at 31–39 East Fourth Street, it became a very popular dining spot from the 1940s until it closed in 1967. The dining room was covered in Rookwood tile with a Dutch windmill theme and could service twenty-five thousand people per day. The restaurant was divided into two sections. The main dining room was finished in Rookwood wall tile in blue, black and gray. There was also a clock and fountain of tile, and twenty-one panels depicting Dutch life and scenery were placed about the restaurant.

Adjoining the main dining room was the cafeteria line, where customers chose their food, decorated in light glazed wall tile with a border of Rookwood *faience* tile. The décor was so valued that when the restaurant closed, the Rookwood tiles were removed and sold piece by piece at auction. One of the Dutch scenic panels of a peasant woman and her young daughter walking toward a windmill was donated to the Cincinnati Art Museum. Recognizable from the outside with its neon rotating windmill sign, Mills was a great, affordable, casual spot to have lunch while shopping or taking in a movie in downtown Cincinnati's heyday.

The Wheel

Founded in 1901, the Wheel Café at 537 Walnut, near Fountain Square, was co-owned by Meyer Silverglade and his son-in-law, Fisher Bacharach. They employed Dave Reinhart as manager in the 1910s. Silverglade was president of the Crown Brewery and also owned the Hub Café around the corner. The Wheel was one of the largest and most prosperous saloons in the city before Prohibition. Pre-Prohibition Cincinnati beer barons often owned cafés to guarantee sales of their beer. After Prohibition, the Wheel was updated with modern equipment and made into an upscale restaurant. Meyer's son, Abe, took over proprietorship in the 1920s and for the Hotel Walton. During Abe's watch, he expanded the cigar and tobacco department, making it a much more important part of the business, to make up for lost liquor sales. What follows is an excerpt from the book *Cincinnati: A Guide to the Queen City and Its Neighbors*, which describes the day Prohibition began at the Wheel:

> *On May 26, 1919, local bars and beer parlors accommodated overflow crowds. All day and well into the evening men drank at their favorite saloons, a little stunned by the fact that the next day would bring prohibition. Everywhere the cash registers snapped with staccato rings; in some places trade ran to $20,000.*
>
> *As the closing hour drew near, an* Enquirer *reporter was on hand to record the historic moment.*
>
> *Midnight in front of the Wheel Café resembled the old Klondyke days…Two hundred men, each carrying a battle, a jug, or a case of liquor, thronged the barroom.*
>
> *Fisher Bacharach, the manager, stood on the table. Coatless, and with sleeves rolled up, he waved his left hand filled with bills of all denominations. "The town is dry," he announced. "Outside everybody," he commanded.*
>
> *And so, at 12:01 o'clock, Cincinnati…passed into the shadow of the valley of ice cream and ginger ale.*

Despite its efforts to stay afloat during Prohibition making soft drinks, the Crown Brewery closed in 1925. But the Wheel Café stayed in business. Fast-forward to 1933, and the Wheel Café figured historically in Cincinnati when Prohibition was repealed, becoming the first establishment to receive a shipment of beer on April 7, from Bruckmann Brewery in Cumminsville, the only Cincinnati brewery to remain open during Prohibition. A firsthand account of that day from a bartender, Mr. McCullough, from the book *Over the Barrel: The Brewing History and Beer Culture of Cincinnati* by Timothy Holian, notes:

> *People lined up 10 to 15 deep on Walnut Street between Fifth and Sixth, just waiting to get in to get a taste. We didn't figure they'd do much eating, so we almost did away with the platter lunches. The only food we served was sandwiches which were wrapped ahead of time….We had only the lower floor open when they started packing in. There were at least nine bartenders on the job. Soon [I was sent] upstairs to open up another bar on the second floor. At both bars we would set up a barrel of beer…open the spigot and let it run. We never had to shut off the spigot, so fast did that beer move. We just shoved the half-liter and liter glasses and mugs across*

A postcard that shows the exterior of the Wheel Café in its heyday. *Courtesy of Don Prout, Cincinnati Views.*

the bars. [The customers] *would toss their money on the bar, grab a beer and stand aside. We would throw the money into the open register. It went on like that all day.*

The Wheel Café remained open into the 1980s, after it had moved to Sixth and Main, making it one of the longest-running cafés in Cincinnati that survived Prohibition.

Chirping at the Cricket

The ownership of the Cricket Restaurant in the Palace Hotel is a rags-to-riches immigrant story. Herman Elsaesser, the hero of the story, was born in Baden, Germany, in 1863. At age eighteen, during Otto Von Bismarck's imperial reign, he fled the country. In search of work to support his mother, he decided to settle in Cincinnati. Penniless, hungry and forced to sleep in a box in an alleyway, Herman asked for help, either food or a job, at the newly built Palace Hotel. When the supervisor turned him away, Herman vowed that he would someday own his own restaurant, maybe even the Palace Hotel. Herman eventually found work in a bakery and later bought his own bakery/restaurant. By 1927, he had saved enough money to buy the Palace Hotel (now the Cincinnatian Hotel and Cricket). He ordered his employees never to turn away a hungry person.

Built in 1882, the eight-story Palace Hotel was designed in French Second Empire style and was the tallest building in Cincinnati. The hotel had three hundred guest rooms and a shared bathroom at either end of each corridor. The Palace Hotel was proud to provide elevators and incandescent lighting. It also had hitching posts along the front of the hotel and was strategically located in the heart of the city where the trolley cars made their turns. The Cricket was the only restaurant in the Palace and has remained very popular well into the twentieth century.

The Palace Hotel became the Cincinnatian Hotel in the 1950s. In 1983, the hotel closed for four years and $25 million of renovation, reopening in 1987 as the grand hotel it is now. The beautiful atrium topped with a vast skylight was created in the renovation, and a hotel that once held three hundred rooms now has half that number in order to accommodate larger guest rooms with private baths. The historic exterior was preserved in the renovation.

An anniversary placemat of the Cricket shows various views and faces over the years. *Courtesy of the Public Library of Cincinnati and Hamilton County.*

Herman and his wife, Petronella, settled with their ten children in Price Hill. In 1929, Herman bought a 250-acre dairy farm "out in the country." His son Steve, blind since infancy, operated the farm for many years. In 1949, Herman's youngest son, Bill, transformed the dairy farm into a "party barn" and carried on his parents' legacy of home-style food and service. Bill died in 1984, but his wife, Dolores, still keeps the farm, one of the most popular places to have a party in Cincinnati.

WASHINGTON PLATFORM

Washington Platform was built on the Miami-Erie Canal in 1860 by Johan Armleder as his Wine and Lager Beer saloon. The Wurtemburg-German immigrant boarded and fed folks until his death in 1872.

The next owner, Fiedel Bader, named the building Washington Platform in 1875 and operated it until 1882. A line of other owners followed, but in 1912, John Hauck Brewing Company bought the business and continued to operate it as the Washington Platform until Prohibition in 1919.

In 1986, John Diebold took over as chef and, in 1988, became owner at the age of twenty-four, reestablishing the Washington Platform Saloon and Restaurant. Today, the restaurant is part of Cincinnati's proud heritage, serving delicious and fresh seafood dishes and other down-home southern cooking. It has a popular oyster fest every spring, this year being its twenty-ninth annual event, keeping the tradition of Cincinnati's love affair with the oyster. It's a great place to dine before going to an event at Music Hall or one of the many theaters nearby.

Hathaway's

Hathaway's Coffee Shop in the Carew Tower Arcade has been serving Cincinnatians breakfast and lunch for more than fifty-nine years. Founded by Lloyd Hathaway in 1956, it was the most beloved venture of the fourteen restaurants he owned. Nicknamed "Torchy" because of his red hair, Hathaway came to Cincinnati from the Northeast to open a Minute Chef restaurant—an early fast-food eatery—for the Sheraton Hotel Corporation. He also owned Hathaway's Fountain Plaza Cafeteria in the Terrace Hilton Hotel, Lloyd's One East on Vine Street and Lloyd's in Madeira.

The Emery family built the Art Deco Carew Tower and Netherland Hilton Hotel complex in 1930, at the beginning of the Depression. It opened with seven restaurants: the feature Restaurant Continentale; the Arcadia Tea Room; the Rotisserie Grill; a luncheonette; the Frontier Room; the Pavilion Caprini, a big-band nightclub where Doris Day made her professional debut; and a coffee shop.

The classic mid-century diner features black-and-white checkered tile, a long winding counter with aqua stools, aqua banquettes and beehive-sporting waitresses in '50s-style dresses. For breakfast, you can order an assortment of eggs, meat, goetta, toast and pancakes, like the famous banana pancakes. For lunch, you can have club sandwiches, homemade chicken noodle soup or a variety of burgers, salads and other unique sandwiches. Also known for its rich, hand-dipped milkshakes and a full soda fountain, it's a great place to step back in time and sip on a treat with a sweatheart.

Lloyd met his wife, Vera, "at the counter," and they would be together for fifty-seven years. Both retired from the restaurant in 1996, but their tradition lives on.

DOING THE BUNNY-HOP DOWNTOWN

Many new to Cincinnati don't know that we had a Playboy Club downtown from 1964 to 1983. In the eighth floor of the Executive Building at 35 East Seventh Street, it added a posh entertainment and dining element to our city. The complex included the Living Room, which had a buffet and the

THE **PLAYBOY CLUB**

DISTINGUISHED CLUBS IN MAJOR CITIES

A Cincinnati Playboy bunny ascends the staircase of the Playboy Club to the Penthouse. *Courtesy of the Public Library of Cincinnati and Hamilton County.*

Playmate Bar. The Party Room could be rented to host private parties out of the public eye. But it was the Penthouse where most of the action at the club took place. With a $2.50 cover charge, it was where the "bunnies" served sirloin steak and the finest filet mignon until 1:30 a.m. The Penthouse also featured top comedy, variety and vocal acts every day. With headliners like Redd Foxx, Flip Wilson and a young Jay Leno, it felt like a slice of Las Vegas in Cincinnati.

But the real draw was the bunnies. More than 150 women donned cuffs, oversized bunny tails, ears and three-inch heels to serve drinks and food during the club's nineteen-year run. One of the first Cincinnati Playboy bunnies, Betty Miller, wrote a book about her experience there called *Storms Never Last: Memoirs of a Playboy Bunny*. Hired by Hugh Hefner's brother, Keith, she found the world at the Cincinnati Playboy Club to be full of glamour, glitz and excitement. But life as a Playboy bunny wasn't as easy as people might think, Miller described. The girls were on call at all times and couldn't eat anything before their shifts started. That was probably wise, as it took two people to pin girls into their bunny costumes, which Miller noted were uncomfortable and hard to breathe in.

When Playboy Club's format changed to disco in 1976, its glory days faded. After several liquor violations and a steady decline in business, the Cincinnati Playboy Club closed in September 1983.

Chapter 6

UPTOWN RESTAURANTS

While the downtown core was the center of Cincinnati fine dining, the suburb of Clifton has been the home of many classic restaurants too, with its proximity to the University of Cincinnati, Hebrew Union College and several hospitals. Farther out into some of the older suburbs, like Glendale, even more classic restaurants have also been delighting patrons for decades.

BUSY BEE

The Busy Bee, owned by Joe Gocker, was the neighborhood restaurant on Ludlow Avenue. A great place for drinks and dinner, it also showcased live entertainment on the weekends in the 1950s and 1960s.

Food was good and reasonable, served with miniature loaves of bread like those served at the Maisonette. Some said that it was a cocktail lounge so dark inside that it made the fried chicken invisible. Known for that fried chicken and onion rings, the Busy Bee also served steaks, hamburgers and seafood. It was the favorite bar of local writer Jonathon Valin's fictional detective Harry Stone.

There were three waves of customers: the old ladies who came in between 5:30 p.m. and 6:00 p.m., the dinner crowd of slightly younger couples and, finally, the singles, students and leftovers of Clifton after dark.

"*See you at the Bee—a familiar saying on the U.C. Campus for years*"

BUSY BEE

316 Ludlow Ave.   AVon 9038

An advertisement from the University of Cincinnati yearbook shows sweethearts choosing a jukebox song at the Busy Bee. *Courtesy of University of Cincinnati Library.*

Jerry Stall took ownership in the late 1980s, updating it into a lighter '50s diner with '80s touches, integrating vinyl booths and pop art of the era. After closing, the Thai Café moved into its place in 1998.

Vernon Manor Hotel

The Vernon Manor hotel, built in 1924, provided general lodging and dining to the public. Modeled after the Hatfield House in Hertfordshire, England, it became *the* place to stay for traveling musicians and notable people. The Beatles, Bob Dylan, Willie Nelson, Kenny Chesney and Presidents Kennedy and Johnson all stayed at Vernon Manor.

By 1945, when Walter Schott, Red's owner Marge Schott's father-in-law, acquired the hotel, it was in decline, but he renovated to its former glory. In the 1960s and 1970s, the neighborhood continued to decline, forcing it to be sold in 1977, when 80 percent of the residents were low-income permanent residents, and then again in 1986 to the Belvedere Corporation.

The hotel featured the Forum Grill for fine dining, described as having a moose lodge interior, and the Cardigan's Café, its English pub, for drinks, specially priced hors d'oeuvres, an extended dinner menu and live entertainment on weekends. The other dining rooms included the Grand Regency Ballroom, the intimate Oak Room and the Rooftop Garden. It also had large meeting and banquet space for social gatherings and weddings.

In 1999, more renovations included an expanded restaurant and bar. Vernon Manor remained open another ten years, closing on March 31, 2009. Its Sunday brunch remained an award-winning tradition in its last years.

Inn the Wood

Bill Wood, the owner of Inn the Wood, originally owned a sub sandwich shop on McMillen in the 1970s. In about 1977, he moved the shop a few doors down on McMillan next to the Bearcat Café and, finally, after marrying Diane in 1979, moved to the large building at 277 Calhoun Street. That building housed an outside bar and a basement bar, and the Woods expanded the menu.

Brunches at Inn the Wood were legendary for UC students and nursed many hangovers from the previous night at the bar. It was where many would celebrate a post-exam victory with its two-egg omelet it called the Peterson Special or with its signature potato crisp—a thin rolled potato pancake of crispy hash browns, enfolding melted cheese, bacon, sautéed onions and sour cream.

Bill and Diane Wood enjoyed much success with their restaurant, earning several awards. But it became a victim of the Clifton Revitalization Project

The building that once housed Inn the Wood on Calhoun Street in Clifton is now demolished. *Author's collection.*

at the university, where virtually all the buildings between McMillan and Calhoun Streets were demolished for new student housing and national chain restaurants.

Keystone Restaurant in Covington, Kentucky, and Hyde Park East in Cincinnati carry the Inn the Wood potato crisp tradition alive, in original and vegetarian form, on their menus in honor of the university landmark.

ZINO'S

The Humphrey family opened the first Zino's restaurant in 1965 in Norwood. More followed in Clifton, Hyde Park, Short Vine, Kenwood Mall, Milford and Walnut Hills. Zino's Firehouse in Short Vine was one of the

This 1960s University of Cincinnati *News Record* ad shows the other Zino's locations in town that delivered. *Courtesy of University of Cincinnati Library.*

more popular of the locations. Its iconic menu item the Zinover was a deep-fried pizza turnover, like a calzone, filled with cheese, marinara sauce and choice of other ingredients.

The restaurants closed in the mid-1990s, but John Humphrey, who grew up working at his parents' restaurants, is bringing back the Zinover after twenty-five years with his food truck the Zinomobile. The food truck's menu will also feature a few other items from the original Zino's restaurants, like its hot brown, eggplant parmesan and Hungarian chicken soup.

RHINE ROOM

The Rhine Room in Tangeman Hall at the University of Cincinnati was a more than forty-year-old institution to students. It was established decades before the fast-food chains that now dot the university. Walls were filled with old photos of students, old paintings and other student memorabilia. An old food hall with round tables perfect for euchre and bridge, it was a great place to hang out, with good thin-crust pizza and local beer. It closed in 2001 when Tangeman Hall was remodeled.

MR. JIM'S STEAKHOUSE

Jim Laverty founded Mr. Jim's Steakhouse in 1963 in Roselawn on Reading Road. Ten more steakhouses were eventually opened across Ohio and Kentucky, to include Louisville, Lexington, Dayton and Cincinnati. His first wife, Maggie, often worked alongside him at the restaurants. She brought the children along with her to help butter garlic bread or cut berries for the fresh pies.

In 1971, Laverty opened the Mr. Jim's Steakhouse on the University of Cincinnati campus. Jim created a place at UC where students loved to eat and hang out. His menus always contained fresh meats, salads, desserts and great coffee. It also had at least eight different homemade soups daily, like oxtail, and a grill for burgers, chicken and pork sandwiches.

When the Tangeman Hall Mr. Jim's closed in 2004, chef Terry and his brothers, John and Tom, reopened in West Harrison, Indiana, in the fall of 2005. Their father, Jim Laverty, the original Mr. Jim, died in 2000.

Shipley's

Shipley's at 214 West McMillan opened in 1928 and was a favorite place for a good sandwich, beer and weighty discussion among UC students and nurses from Good Samaritan and Deaconess Hospitals. Dick Meyer bought the restaurant in 1984, after the former owners had been evicted in 1978 from the McMillan Avenue location, and moved it to Vine Street, where it became more of a club showcasing live music. The Vine Street location was the former site of the Bijou/Roxy/Ritz Theatres.

SHIPLEY'S
214 W. McMillan   PA. 2620

This ad for Shipley's is from a University of Cincinnati yearbook; UC students made up a majority of its patrons. *Courtesy of the University of Cincinnati Library.*

Dana Gardens

If UC has its long-standing student hangouts, Xavier University has one to mention. Dana Gardens, aka "Dana's," has been a popular hangout for Xavier students, faculty and alumni since 1938. The perfect place to take in a basketball game or just drink your cares away, it's like walking into an XU grad's basement. Dana's serves up food such as the "U.C. Sucks Mett," a mettwurst served on two pieces of toast; the "Muskie Burger," with bacon and provolone; and the ultimate drunk food, fresh-cut French fries. For drinks, try Herschel's Special, a mysteriously sweet and potent pink drink created by longtime bartender Herschel. Dana's has made it to number seventy-eight on the list of Best College Bars in the United States.

Grand Finale

The Grand Finale has been a Cincinnati favorite since 1975, owned by Cindy and Larry Youse. After enjoying a nice steak, lamb or seafood, you'd better save room for some delicious pie, cheesecake or cobbler. As the name suggests, it is famous for its desserts. One of its seasonal favorite desserts is Mo's Pumpkin Pie, from a more than eighty-year-old recipe from Larry Youse's mother. For pumpkin pie snobs, it ranks in the realm of Buskin and Frisch's pumpkin pies. Its cinnamon, mace and cloves are balanced so that one doesn't overpower the other. Its light crust is baked into a small crock topped with fresh whipped cream. It is also famous for its extensive brunch buffet, for which it has won many awards.

Antique furnishings of the period of the house fill the restaurant, as do oil paintings by co-owner Cindy Youse. The cuisine is American grill with French accents, most notably the choice of five different crepes as a side dish.

The building, at the crossroads of East Sharon Road and Congress, was originally built in about 1875. In 1906, John J. Kelly bought the building at a sheriff's auction and opened it as a saloon and grocery. It fronted the main road from Dayton to Cincinnati and was a big draw for travelers. Liquor sparked bar brawls on occasion, and one man was shot and killed in the front-room bar. In 1930, Kelly built an addition, from which his sisters Emma and Rose operated a grocery and lived upstairs. The sisters died in 1970, leaving the building empty for five years until the Youses bought it.

Once a roadside saloon, the Grand Finale is one of Cincinnati's favorite restaurants, especially for its desserts. *Author's collection.*

In the early days, the nighttime baking crew would report strange noises and strange occurrences, like chairs rearranging themselves, hair being pulled and knives flying across the kitchen. Someone suggested that the Grand Finale ghost might have been of a younger member of the original Kelly family.

Iron Horse at the Rails

One handsome two-story brick building, originally known as Bracker's Tavern, has been a landmark in Glendale's Village Square since 1856. During Prohibition, it became a restaurant in the front, with slot machines and liquor in the back. The restaurant and soda fountain, which served French Bauer ice cream, gave a cover for what was really going on. The tavern even delivered breakfast to those who spent a night in the local jail nearby.

In the 1920s, Lilian Bracker, daughter of the owners, and husband Robert Heine installed the soda fountain, sold penny candy and opened for lunch to serve hot soup and sandwiches.

In 1962, Lilian Heine sold to William McConnell and three investors, and they renamed it the Iron Horse Inn after the 1856 steam engine that came through on the rails nearby. In 1971, ownership changed again, to Robert and Vera Mahoney. Then, in 1984, Dewy and Betty Huff took the reins. They elevated the food to scratch cooking with specialties like roast duckling and orange sauce and chicken breast with chicken mousse and julienne vegetables. Bavarian Mud Pie was the favorite dessert. The Iron Horse became a memorable dining experience for the next twenty-three years.

In 1994, the Huffs sold to four local brothers—Ed, William, Robert and Henry Sawyer—who spent several years completely renovating the place. They created two dining rooms, a formal one on the first floor and a less casual tavern-like second-floor dining room. With chef Ron Wise, they added classic choices with contemporary twists, like grilled walleye and mac and cheese, as well as a variety of vegetarian options. Their bread pudding dessert became a favorite.

The Iron Horse changed owners again in 2008 to Robin Thomas, but he sold in 2012 to Ashley and Jay Silbermann, who operated it until 2014 as the Rail House. The historic building now awaits a new birth with new owners.

Let's Meet at the Wigwam

For almost eight decades, family-owned Shuller's Wigwam at 6210 Hamilton Avenue in College Hill was one of the city's most loved restaurants. Founded in 1922 by Russian Jewish immigrants Max and Anna Shuller, it was immediately successful. From humble beginnings as a six-stool hamburger stand next to the Paragon Gas Station, it expanded in

A 1920s photo of the original Shuller's Wigwam at 6210 before its expansion to a modern one-thousand-seat restaurant. *Courtesy of Terry Mecheau.*

1934 with a glass-enclosed biergarten and in 1941 with the unique teepee-shaped building that gave it the "Wigwam" nickname. In 1954, the teepee was demolished and replaced with the modern restaurant building, with two public dining rooms and twelve private party rooms that, combined, made the one-thousand-seat restaurant one of the largest in Cincinnati. It has been a favorite site for reunions of all kinds, wedding receptions, family events and sports banquets. It was even the site of broadcasts by Jean "Shep" Shepherd for WSAI Cincinnati, a storyteller and radio personality best known for scripting and narrating the movie *A Christmas Story*, based on his life growing up in Hammond, Indiana.

During the Depression, Shuller lost six other diners that he had around Cincinnati, including one at Seventh and Vine downtown, but he kept the Wigwam. The Wigwam created an American Indian theme for the menu and featured good solid American fare. In the 1960s, some of these menu items included the Mohican French-fried Seafood Platter Deluxe for $3.25 and the twelve-ounce Squaw Steak Special for $4.75 for "ladies and those who prefer a smaller steak." It was known for its complimentary relish tray of chopped liver, beer cheese, pickled herring and a good and crunchy sauerkraut, as well as its dill bread and onion soup. Also known in later years for its peanut butter pie and a wide variety of imported beers, Shuller's had a little something for everyone.

Max passed on the business to his sons Leo and Saul. Saul loved sports of all kinds, and the family supported the Cincinnati Royals, a former NBA

This 1960s photo shows the inside of the new lounge at Shuller's Wigwam, with Leo Shuller at the table. *Courtesy of Ken Shuller.*

franchise, with a yearly party at the Wigwam. Many patrons had been coming to the restaurant for decades. They had charmed girlfriends over malts and grilled cheese and later talked business over steak and martinis. Even later, they came with their friends, eating turkey croquettes and sipping glasses of Blue Nun.

An interesting set of patrons came to Shuller's every year in January to celebrate the mediocrity of Millard Fillmore, the thirteenth president of the United States. The group's more than one hundred members, called the "Fillmorons," wined and dined on chopped liver and other home-style favorites. Jerry Springer emceed their first annual event in 1980. Other famous patrons to the Wigwam included Ronald Reagan, Doris Day, Perry Como and Woody Hayes.

The children of the loyal patrons, Gen-Xers, did not follow their parents and grandparents to Shuller's. Workers began to have less time for lunch, but Shuller's still thrived on its retiree business. While major highways separated

Shuller's from much of the Greater Cincinnati population, a proximity to four retirement homes delivered loyal customers.

In 1997, after considering expansion and trying to bring younger clientele in, it became apparent to Leo that his son and nephew were not interested in carrying on the business. Leo decided to shut down in 2000, and the building was demolished in 2006. The site remains vacant today, a standing tribute to one of Cincinnati's longest-running family restaurants.

THE GRILL NEXT DOOR ON THE AVENUE

Just around the corner from Shuller's, Bacall's Café has been a neighborhood meeting place since 1982, owned by Jody Williamson. Now the only location, there were once many locations throughout the city. By 1985, there was an Eastside location on Wooster Road and a Mainville location in addition to the College Hill location. Downtown Seventh Street, Glenway Avenue, Beechmont Avenue and Ormond Beach, Florida, locations were added by 1988. Two more were added in 1989: Montgomery Road and Fort Thomas, Kentucky.

Moderately priced food in an Art Deco setting makes this a comfortable lunch or dinner spot. Its signature onion straws come with most of its sandwiches, like its reubens, burgers, wraps and hoagies. It also has an extensive martini menu, featuring the Pomegranate or the Lemon Drop.

VINTAGE CHINESE

Chung Ching is a truly vintage Chinese restaurant. It's a dying breed among all the fused-beyond-recognition Chinese restaurants that throw a bit of everything on their menus. Owned by Joyce Yang and her husband, Steve, they have been offering Cantonese cuisine since 1982, with a few spicy Szechuan dishes thrown in. It sits in a 1930s-era business strip at 5842 Hamilton Avenue in College Hill. The décor may be dated, but the atmosphere is authentic. You can tell its flavors are authentic by the number of Chinese faces seen and languages being spoken inside. Most of the menu items are under ten dollars, and in addition to the menu, you can order off menu. One of the popular items is a vegetable and meat dish that uses a green

Chinese vegetable called "schwe-di-hong," with other seasonal vegetables as available. If you just order "chop-chop," Joyce will know what you mean. The hot and sour soup is very good, and the Governor's Chicken is even spicier than the General Tsao's Chicken. There are so many regulars that Chung Ching doesn't really need to advertise. Most of its regulars would prefer it to remain as it is—one of Cincinnati's best-kept secrets.

The Windjammer

One of the most unique dining experiences in Cincinnati was offered at the Windjammer Restaurant on Chester Road in Sharonville. Opened as an upscale supper club in 1966 by developer Robert Harpenau, it sat next to a Howard Johnson's motel. The restaurant was a ship modeled after an eighteenth-century Spanish galleon, the *El Enfante*, which foundered off the coast of the Florida Keys in a 1733 hurricane. It was part of a fleet bringing treasures from Mexico to Spain. The interior of the restaurant was decorated with artifacts salvaged from the *Enfante* and other similar ships, including its twenty-foot-tall, three-ton anchor. Cannons heavy with encrustation were displayed throughout the restaurant.

The restaurant could handle up to 260 seats for banquets, luncheons and conferences, with two private meeting rooms. Most of the staff were long-timers, and the Windjammer was known for its friendly and professional service.

The original menu specialized in seafood flown in from the major coastlines. Live Maine lobster, Gulf shrimp, frogs' legs, pompano, snapper, sole and a variety of shellfish platters were on the menu. Other turf-based items like New York strip, filet mignon, baby-back ribs and chicken and veal rounded out the menu.

After thirty years, the Windjammer closed on March 28, 1997, and was demolished in 2002. No such dining experience has come close in Cincinnati since the Windjammer.

Windjammer Crab and Corn Fritters

¼ pound all-purpose flour
2 tablespoons baking powder
3 large eggs
8 ounces whole kernel corn, drained, with liquid reserved
1 pound crabmeat
2 ounces jalapeño peppers, diced fine
¼ cup red peppers, diced fine
¼ cup onions, minced
¼ cup celery, diced fine
2 tablespoons Worcestershire sauce
peanut oil

Sift flour and baking powder. Whip the eggs. Add half the corn liquid to eggs. Combine the egg and flour mix, adding all remaining ingredients. Heat the peanut oil to 350 degrees Fahrenheit in a skillet. Drop tablespoon-sized portions of the batter into the hot oil. Fry golden brown, 4–5 minutes. Serve with cocktail sauce and fresh lemon.

Chapter 7

EASTSIDE RESTAURANTS

Fewer longtime restaurants exist on the Eastside compared to the Westside. The Eastside is more in tune with food trends and has more ethnic restaurants than the Westside, and it tends to have fewer neighborhood family restaurants. Hyde Park and Mount Lookout Square, O'Bryanville, Montgomery and Blue Ash go through new restaurants every several years. As discriminating as the Eastside palate seems to be, the oldest are still standard family restaurants with American comfort food.

SKY GALLEY

One Eastside restaurant follows the birth of commercial air flight. That's Sky Galley on Wilmer Avenue, in the old Art Deco Passenger Terminal at Lunken Airport. Sky Galley has welcomed pilots and local diners since the terminal was completed in 1937. It also prepared the inflight foods for American Airlines, which got its start at Lunken Airport, under the name Sky Chef. Customers would get boxes of crispy fried chicken during their flights.

The restaurant is a throwback to when air travel was more relaxing and civilized than it is today. You feel like you might bump into Charles Lindbergh, who landed at Lunken in 1927 to refuel. Inside, a large picture window allows you to dine and enjoy the view of planes landing and taking

The vintage neon sign outside Sky Galley points to its history. *Author's collection.*

off from Lunken's airfield. In warmer weather, you can sit on the patio, within spitting distance of the runways, and experience the sounds and smells of the planes more intimately. A 1930s yellow neon sign advertises the restaurant from the roadside. Enter the main entrance to the terminal and you are surrounded by the history of flight at Lunken, with photos and an Aeronca C-2 aircraft suspended from the ceiling.

Purchased by Kirby Brakvill in 2000, Sky Galley features a diner menu, continuing the tradition of its "World Famous Chicken Livers," which have been served since its opening in 1937. Renamed "Wings" for a brief period from 1995 to 2000, when Dick Duvall owned the restaurant, the current owner has brought it back to its original theme. Other menu items include pulled pork, meatloaf, baby-back ribs and a Cincinnati German favorite, the braunschweiger sandwich, a chicken liver pâté served with spicy mustard. There's something for everyone, from munchies like nachos to higher-end fare like the New York Strip.

Zip's

In a strip of businesses in Mount Lookout Square, there is a landmark burger joint well known to locals: Zip's, "Home of the Girth Burger." It has been serving neighbors here since 1926. Originally owned by Donald and Genevive Karchner, it changed ownership in the 1950s and was owned by Harold Stumpf. At the beginning of 2015, eighteen-year owner Brian Murrie gave over the reins of ownership to longtime general manager Mike Burke, who has been managing Zip's since 2005.

Loyal customers can still order the Girth Burger, a Zip's burger with a split mett from Avril-Bleh meats on Court Street. It was named after Bengals punter Pat McInally, a regular at the burger joint in the 1980s. They can also still enjoy the Train Wreck, a Zip's burger with shaved ham, grilled mett and three types of cheese, as well as other menu standards like its super-crispy onion rings.

Vintage golf clubs and cricket bats hang on the walls, while a classic toy train makes its way around a ceiling track backed by a mural of the businesses on Mount Lookout Square. Upon entering the saloon doors, you can choose a booth or table in the one large dining room. On weekends, come in before 11:00 a.m. if you don't want to wait. There's

Zip's menu shows the original owners in a loving pose. *Courtesy of Zip's.*

a discreet bar in the back guarded by a second set of saloon doors where you might see Nick Lachey enjoying a burger or waiting for a carryout order.

Arthur's

Just off Hyde Park Square is Arthur's, a neighborhood favorite. The location on Edwards Road was originally named Allen E. Bradford Restaurant in 1947. It transitioned to Apke's Grill the next year and then Art's in 1956. Finally, in the 1970s, Arthur's became what it is today. Current owners Susan Selzer, Joe Santorelli and B.J. Hughes began working at Arthur's in the early 1990s as bussers and servers while in college. They eventually ended up managing the restaurant for many years before buying it from their bosses. The restaurant is split into three dining rooms: an open room with tables in front of an ornate antique mahogany bar taken from an old hotel in Louisville, Kentucky; a side room with booths; and a New Orleans–inspired

Arthur's off Hyde Park Square is a neighborhood favorite. *Author's collection.*

outdoor terrace. Across from the bar is a giant wall mural of former bar regulars painted by cartoonist Jerry Dowlin. With award-winning items like a beer-battered cod sandwich, fried cheese and a variety of burgers, it has developed a loyal following in the Eastside neighborhoods.

The Echo

Just next door to Arthur's is another longtime neighborhood favorite, the Echo Restaurant. Known for serving hearty, home-cooked fare at reasonable prices, it has a family diner feel, with a teardrop counter and cozy booths. Louise Schwartz opened the Echo in 1945 as a sandwich shop.

Louise expanded in 1975, making "the back room" from a former laundry. Over the following years, business thrived for the Echo. Sassy female waitresses served generations of customers. However, in 1978, a kitchen fire damaged the restaurant, causing it to be closed temporarily.

Louise sold the restaurant in 1989 after forty-four years of ownership. Two owners followed over the next six years until, in 1995, it was purchased by Stephanie Surgeon, who took the Echo into the next generation. She kept the pies made from Louise's original recipes and a commitment to home-cooked food at fair prices. Some changes were made, however, like opening

Echo has been a standard on Edwards Avenue for more than seventy years. *Author's collection.*

on Sunday, which has become the busiest day of the week. But others, like the diner-style counter and stools, remained.

The clientele is evolving from the most loyal elderly patrons to college kids looking for a hangover cure and school kids with parents or with friends. Lunch patrons include anyone from judges to hardworking moms.

The breakfast items are seasonal and can include pumpkin pie pancakes or spring chicken salad. And to satisfy the true Cincinnatian, a side of goetta can be ordered with any item.

THE ESTABLISHMENT

If there's a bar that makes you forget what side of town you're on, it's the Establishment. Owned by Jim Klei, it was established in 1969. Its laidback, casual atmosphere is what brings its patrons back, as well as its sandwiches—Texas toast grilled cheese, turkey and corned beef reubens, grilled chicken, hoagies and fish. Affectionately known as "the E" to regulars, it attracts a crowd from both sides of town. With its gray brick walls and windowless exterior, it may make you think it's a strip club. But come on, it's in Oakley on Wasson Avenue—it couldn't be. Its American pub food menu includes stuffed potato skins, Buffalo wings, chicken tenders, corn dogs and mozzarella sticks and can be eaten inside or on the back patio.

SHAKING THE HABIT

Habits Café is a great neighborhood bar and grill located in the heart of Oakley Square. Prior to being Habits, it was the Old Lenox Grill in the early 1900s and then Luke's Lounge. Owner Mark Rogers has been serving hamburgers, fish and chips and great sandwiches since 1980. He expanded the restaurant next door into what was a retail store. Get any of these items with its signature potato rags or famous white chicken chili and wash them down with one of ninety bottled beers or a cocktail from the friendly bar. The potato rag is a mound of shredded potatoes slathered with bacon, tomatoes, onions, cheeses and ranch dressing—not for those watching their cholesterol. With an outside patio that overlooks the activity going on in Oakley Square, Habits has become a neighborhood landmark.

In addition to its food and friendly service, Habits has also been in the news for its stories of the supernatural. Apparently, the ghost of a policeman killed on site haunts the basement beneath the restaurant. But Rogers is used to ghosts. He also owns the 20th Century Theatre across Oakley Square from Habits, now a concert and events venue. It, too, is rumored to be haunted by a ghost, that of a former movie projectionist.

SALEM GARDENS

Salem Gardens is a legendary Anderson Township bar and grill that has been in business since 1926. Called the "Friendly Corner" by locals, it's situated on the corner of Salem Road and Beacon Street. It's an unpretentious local watering hole with great food. Current owner Mike Larkin, an Anderson Township native and McNicholas High School grad, and his wife, Judy, have owned the bar and grill since 1983. You might call it the Eastside version of Price Hill Chili, as many groups like the McNicholas High School Alumni have their monthly meetings here. It even has its own recipe for Cincinnati chili and cheese coneys, which probably has its roots in the Gold Star chili formula; Gold Star was founded not far away from Salem Gardens in Mount Washington in 1965. Salem Gardens has won awards for its burgers and wings but also features double-deckers, healthy salads and homemade chili. It has some great fried items like spicy pickles and beer-battered button mushrooms. In warmer weather, patrons can enjoy a large patio in the back, and inside are an old shuffleboard game free to patrons, a long bar with local microbrews on tap and TVs for watching the game.

CELESTIAL VIEWS

The Celestial and Rookwood Pottery were owned by Joseph Rippe Sr. for nearly thirty years. He bought both buildings and restaurants in 1977. The Celestial has undeniably the best view in Cincinnati—a view that patrons of the Highland House shared more than one hundred years ago. But it has also struggled with its identity. It has gone from old-school heavy American fare to French to American steakhouse. However, that hasn't stopped it from being the center of many family celebrations, from anniversaries to high school and college dances.

Around 2000, Rippe went about a much-needed updating of both restaurants. By that time, most Cincinnatians had already said goodbye to heavy cream sauces and beef Wellington, and its dated concept was losing clientele. Rippe hired chef Tsvik "Vik" Silverburg to come in and revamp the Celestial as a high-class French restaurant.

Chanaka de Lanerolle bought the restaurant from Rippe in 2004. He also owned Teak Thai and the Mount Adams Fish House. In 2005, with new chef Scott Niedhard, De Lanerolle turned what was a French restaurant into a steakhouse with a contemporary twist. Niedhard added dishes like veal chop dusted with Chinese five-spice and venison chops with cranberry mint glaze. The Celestial Steakhouse remains, with a strong menu of steaks, seafood and, of course, the best view in Cincinnati.

ROOKWOOD POTTERY

The Rookwood Pottery sits on the peaks of Mount Adams in the historic property of a beloved Cincinnati art pottery. Founded in 1880 by the wealthy and sassy Maria Longworth, the granddaughter of millionaire Nicholas Longworth, it remained a pottery until 1967.

It became a restaurant in 1977 under ownership of Joseph Rippe Sr., who also owned the Highland Tower and its restaurant, the Celestial, next door. He inserted novelty tables into the old beehive pottery kilns and served burgers and reuben sandwiches with fries like you might find at any American pub.

Then Joe Creighton opened the new Rookwood in 2008 and brought his element of "un-cool industrial handmade experience" to Cincinnati, long before urban hipsters in flannel, ZZ Top beards and overgreased handlebar moustaches started serving "curated cocktails" in Over-the-Rhine. Creighton brought chef-driven comfort foods to the Cincinnati scene, serving items like goetta hanky panky, Grippo's barbecue seasoned fries and the Berkshire Belly, a pork belly sandwich.

Creighton gave the Rookwood a much-needed overhaul, with colors corresponding to old Rookwood pottery pieces, Edison bulbs, dark woods, a nod to the historic and contemporary art. A new two-level exterior porch capitalizes on the beautiful views of downtown and the river, and a sunken fire pit made from foundation stones from the old Mount Adams Incline takes advantage of location. Current chef Jackson Rouse describes the new Rookwood as a "historic hipster paradise."

The owners, Creighton, Joe Mouch and Rom Wells, opened the Cheapside Café, a breakfast and lunch café, in 2014 in the original Spurs nightclub on East Eighth Street and are expanding to a bar this year in Over-the-Rhine on Walnut Street, quickly becoming a force in the Cincinnati food scene.

CITYVIEW TAVERN

In a long, narrow Italianate building on Oregon Street in Mount Adams, next to the right-of-way of the old incline, is one of the few structures on its street that hasn't fallen into the hill. Originally a grocery for the Irish working class of the neighborhood, the site added a saloon in 1901. Capitalizing on the same gorgeous views of the city as the Celestial and Rookwood above it on the hill, only those lucky enough to find a table on the small deck can really enjoy it.

Known today for its great burgers, chili and its killer Bloody Marys rimmed with Old Bay, CityView is a traditional, unpretentious neighborhood bar, with walls filled with Cincinnati memorabilia. Deb Hennigan, its owner since 1985, has left the shelving pine paneling up that previous owners Ted and Myrt Lageman installed.

A local legend notes that CityView doesn't serve tequila because of Charles Manson, who reputedly lived down the street from the bar in the 1960s and threatened to jump off the deck after drinking too much of it.

THE HERITAGE

The Heritage Restaurant on Wooster Pike in Mariemont earned the nickname "the Wildest Game in Town" because of the exotic meats it served. Opened in 1959 in the historic 1827 Edgar Scott home, it was owned by Howard and Jan Melvin.

When the Melvins sold the Heritage in 2004, it had been a restaurant for 101 years already. In 1905, Frank Kelly reopened it as Kelly Gardens. At the time, Wooster Pike was a main thoroughfare into Cincinnati from the east for stagecoaches, wagons and cattle herds. Frank "Pretty" Kelly ran it with Ma Kelly, his wife, until he died in 1919. His son, Cornelius "Corny" Kelly, took over after that. Corny liked to hang out with athletes and prizefighters and was known as a sharp dresser and brawler himself. He brought slot machines into the restaurant and turned it into a real Prohibition-era speakeasy. Federal authorities shut down Kelly Gardens in 1935.

In 1937, after the Ohio River flood cleared, Paul Bowshear bought the site and relocated his restaurant the Cottage there until selling to the Melvins in 1959.

Howard and Jan had both worked for restaurants owned by the Comisar family before opening the Heritage. They always stayed up to date on food trends by traveling around and seeing what other restaurants were trying. The Heritage was cooking Cajun before it became a mega trend. It was also way ahead of the curve when it came to serving nouvelle cuisine, American comfort food, locally grown produce and free-range chicken.

Chef Jerry Hard became proficient at working exotic game like hippo, alligator, elephant, lion, buffalo, bear, venison and pheasant. Its supplier was Zimmer Company in Chicago, Illinois, an exotic meat wholesaler that bought from farmers who were raising these animals for eating. Many patrons looked forward to its annual Fall Wild Game Festival, where these exotic meats were made into exquisite entrées.

The Heritage sat vacant for many years until 2012, when a young group of buddies—Blake Horburgh, brewmaster; Whit Hesser, general manager; and Bobby Slattery, distribution manager—opened it as 50 West, a microbrewery and tapas-style eatery.

SUGAR N' SPICE

In 2015, Sugar n' Spice celebrates its seventy-fifth anniversary. This Paddock Hills diner has been delighting Cincinnati clientele with its secret recipe wispy-thin pancakes, huge fluffy omelettes, signature creative sandwiches and specials since FDR was signing new deals. The breakfast and lunch menu has changed little since Mort Keller established the restaurant in 1941, including the goetta that it serves as a side for breakfast.

Today, Sugar n' Spice prides itself on creating a fun, comfortable, family-friendly atmosphere, serving the same great food that has kept people coming back for generations. The diversity of the cars in the parking lot

Founder Mort Keller and other early workers pose in front of the Sugar n' Spice in 1941. *Courtesy of Cincinnati Views.*

reflects that of the restaurant's patrons. From Ford trucks to BMWs, from college students to grandparents and from construction workers to doctors, people from all walks of life visit Sugar n' Spice on a daily basis.

Steven Frankel is the fifth owner of this landmark but feels he's more the caretaker of a historic icon rather than its owner. He is always working the dining room with samples for those waiting, especially on busy Saturdays, and offering rubber ducks as gifts. What started as a treat for the kids, in Happy Meal mentality, escalated when college students and grandparents began requesting them too. He passes out about one thousand ducks a week now. It's not exactly the most cost-effective gimmick, but it makes the Sugar n' Spice experience unique.

You can get eggs and pancakes anywhere, Frankel said, but people come to Sugar n' Spice for the omelettes, the pancakes and the insanity.

BLUEBIRD

The Bluebird in Norwood has been open since 1970. With a southern diner feel, it serves reasonably priced home-style food, with daily specials and an extensive menu. It's filled with booths, each with its own mini jukebox with songs from the '50s and '60s. It has all the elements of good comfort food—scrambled eggs, goetta, meatloaf sandwiches and burgers. It even has its own recipe for Cincinnati-style chili that it serves on threeways and cheese coneys.

Rocking the Barbecue Since 1951

The Montgomery Inn is a food icon in Cincinnati. When out-of-towners ask where they should eat in Cincinnati, one of the most common responses is the Montgomery Inn Boathouse downtown. It offers a taste of our award-winning Cincinnati-style barbecue ribs and a wonderful view of the Ohio River. Diners walk into the enormous restaurant, see photos of all the many celebrities who have come into the restaurant and get a feel for the "big dreamer" kind of person owner Ted Gregory was. The Ribs King logo shows a profile of Ted with his crown and his signature cigar.

In 1950, Ted Gregory came to Cincinnati at the urging of a pal from Detroit, Michigan, where he grew up. The friend had four blond Greek nieces in the city to whom he wanted to introduce the young and available Gregory. One of them, Matula, became his wife. In November 1951, Ted and Matula Gregory bought McCabe's Inn in Montgomery and renamed it Montgomery Inn. It became a family business, with Ted's parents, Thomas and Tasia; Matula's sister, Tasha; and their father, Charlie Kalomeres, all pitching in at the restaurant, which didn't initially serve its now famous barbecue ribs. Ted knew how precarious the restaurant business was. His Greek immigrant parents ran a small restaurant during the Depression in Detroit and went broke.

It wasn't until the late 1950s that Matula cooked the famous barbecue ribs for Ted and some of his buddies at the bar. They were so well liked that Ted asked Matula if she could re-create them, and he started serving the ribs on Fridays and Saturdays only. They became so popular that by the early 1960s they were a normal menu item, now served with the crispy Saratoga chips. And the fame was sealed when, in 1968, Dale Stevens, food critic for the *Cincinnati Post*, crowned Ted Gregory the "Cincinnati Ribs King."

The next year, Johnny Cash and June Carter performed live for guests in the main dining room. Other celebrities, like Dinah Shore and Bob Hope, visited the Inn, and it became a household name in Cincinnati. Current

The ribs at Montgomery Inn are so juicy and saucy that many, like Flora and Roger Woellert shown here, choose to "grab a bib and dig in." *Author's collection.*

vice-president of the business Evan Andrews said that Bob Hope's visit was the tipping point for Montgomery Inn becoming an iconic brand.

The 1980s saw great expansion for the Gregory family business. They expanded the dining room at the original Inn, opened Montgomery Inn East on Beechmont Avenue and, in 1988, celebrated the groundbreaking of the Boathouse on Eastern Avenue on the Ohio River. The Boathouse debuted to sellout crowds and has become a dining icon for the city, where many families celebrate birthdays, anniversaries and graduations.

In 1994, they started shipping ribs by mail order. Bob Hope had them sent regularly to his house in Palm Springs. By 2001, a new Fort Mitchell, Kentucky location was added, allowing them to produce 13.5 tons of ribs per week and 500,000 gallons of sauce annually. Finally, in 2009, they expanded north and opened the Dublin, Ohio location.

In 2001, the Gregory family lost its patriarch, whose memorial service at St. Nicholas Greek Orthodox Church saw hundreds and required overnight police guarding by Officer Brian Uhl. The restaurant continues to make national news, seeing an award for a top-ten barbecue sauce in the nation, which was given as a fifty-second birthday gift to President Obama. Ted Gregory's legacy lives on in the thousands of vistors his restaurant continues to delight. And Matula's secret sauce lives on under the guardianship of her son-in-law, Evan Andrews.

FOX AND CROW

Newport, Kentucky, wasn't the only place where high rollers went to wager. What is now Johnny and Carlo's on Montgomery Road has gone from farmhouse to speakeasy to gambling casino to legitimate restaurant. Julius Fleischmann, an heir to the Fleischmann Yeast fortune, bought the 1847 farmhouse on Montgomery Road in 1933 and transformed it into the Fox and Crow, one of Cincinnati's poshest supper clubs. It had a French chef and outdoor patio to dance to big bands. The expensive menu included imported caviar and roast duckling.

It changed owners several times in the 1940s, and by 1949, it was owned by an out-of-town syndicate. By then, gambling had been added to the menu. Word got out, and near midnight on December 3, 1949, Hamilton County sheriff Chief Investigator Carl Meyer led a raid on the establishment. The doorman tipped his hat and rang a buzzer, and the deputies went through the front door just in time to see a paneled wall closing to the rear. They broke the locks and found a back room with slot machines, a roulette wheel, a blackjack table with chips up to $1,000 in denomination and twenty patrons trying to pretend that they were playing bridge. Pop star Kitty Kallen kept on singing during the raid, dedicating the song "Mule Train" to Carl Meyer and company.

It remained the Fox and Crow for a total of thirty-eight years, until closing in 1971. It reopened as Charley's Crab in 1973. Once the city's premier seafood spot, it became known as Charley's Oyster Bar and Grille. In the 1970s, it was known to stack up against famous seafood restaurants in other cities like Bookbinders in Philadelphia, Pier 52 in New York City and Anthony's Pier IV in Boston.

In 2001, it became Jeff Ruby's Johnny and Carlo Steakhouse, named after the deputy and sheriff who shut the place down in 1949 for illegal gambling.

Charley's Halibut Forte

7 ounces halibut filet
flour
3 tablespoons butter
2 large shrimp
2 ounces mushrooms, sliced
1 tablespoon scallions, diced
1 teaspoon lemon juice

Dredge the halibut in flour. Sauté in 2 tablespoons of melted butter until both sides are browned. Add the shrimp, mushrooms and scallions. Remove from the pan. Deglaze the pan with the lemon juice. Add remaining butter, melt and serve.

Quatman Café

Each neighborhood has its own café or bar where you can get a good burger and beer and watch a game or connect with friends. Quatman Café in Norwood is one of those family-friendly places. Sitting on Montgomery

A vintage sign beckons customers into the Quatman Café to enjoy one of the best burgers in Cincinnati. *Author's collection.*

A mosaic placed in a spot of honor shows the founder of Quatman's, Albert Imm. *Author's collection.*

Avenue in the shadow of Our Lady of the Holy Spirit Center, it was founded in 1966 by Albert "Albo" Imm (1940–2007) and Ken Talmage. Now owned by Matt Imm, Quatman Café has become a Cincinnati icon known for cheeseburgers, chili, homemade soups and the coldest beer in town. Nestled in a double timber-framed building that looks straight out of Bavaria, the place is laidback, friendly and unassuming. The special—which includes a cheeseburger, a generous portion of French fries and your choice of soda or beer for seven dollars—has to be the best burger deal in town. With your choice of cheese (American, Swiss or cheddar), onion, lettuce and tomato, you get a half-pound burger made of freshly ground chuck care of Wassler's meats, the sole supplier since opening in 1966. Grilled to perfection and just pink enough to be tender and juicy, it's bound to cure any hangover. Quatman's chili is well liked, as is its homemade ham salad, which can be purchased from the deli. Quatman's is so popular that it has opened a second location in Mason, on Main Street, to follow many of its alumni in the migration to the burbs.

Chapter 8

WESTSIDE RESTAURANTS

There's something about the Westside of Cincinnati that seems to make it an incubator for long-lasting restaurants. There's a magic there that food concept inventors would love to bottle. Maybe it's the loyalty of the families on the Westside, who rarely move out of the Catholic parishes where they were raised. For example, someone on the Westside identifies where they live by the parish—"I live in 'Res [Resurrection] but grew up in St. L's [St. Lawrence]."

Westsiders pledge loyalty to restaurants where they can meet after high school football games and after Mass on Sunday. It's not unusual for a family restaurant to be open for more than fifty years and still be operated by the same family. Two well-known chain restaurants—LaRosa's and Skyline—got their start on the Westside. Whatever the magic, there's also something Westside restaurants have in common: they are always involved in their community. Whether it's volunteering at local festivals or donating their food services, they become synonymous with longtime family memories.

SAN ANTONIO, THE PATRON OF CINCINNATI PIZZA CHAINS

On the Westside of Cincinnati is a neighborhood called South Fairmont, or "Little Italy." It was once home to several hundred families of Italian immigrants. They tended vegetable gardens, grapevines, fig trees and chickens in their backyards. Most were Catholic and attended the Italian Catholic parish San Antonio. Like they did in the old country, they paraded the old statue of the Madonna di Constantinopoli, the patroness of fishermen, through the streets on her feast day in July, with fireworks. Those families that could afford it moved up the hill after World War II to Westside neighborhoods of Price Hill, Cheviot and Western Hills but still come back to San Antonio for Sunday Mass and social activities.

San Antonio held a yearly festival to support the church. Along with bratwurst and beer, the San Antonio festival served something most Cincinnatians in the 1950s had never heard of: pizza. In Little Italy, it was common for the older Italian ladies to make pizza for their families at home. At the time in Cincinnati, there were only two pizzerias: Capri Pizza at Tennessee and Reading in Bond Hill, founded in 1949 by Daniel J. Vaccariello, and Pasquale's Pizza, founded by the Gramaglia brothers, both from Little Italy. Pasquale's was the first pizza many Cincinnatians tasted.

A recollection of Dennis Eckhart, who grew up in Little Italy in the 1950s (from his book *Every Life Is a Story and This Is Mine: A Memoir and Recollections*), explains the novelty of pizza at the San Antonio church festival:

> *There was a large kitchen in the basement of the church* [San Antonio]. *During festival time some of the women of the church, Grandma Delseno included, would prepare this pizza. This meant making home-made sauce and preparing the dough from scratch. Some of the younger women would carry it across the street to the festival grounds and sell it. It was 15 cents a slice. A big slice.*
>
> *During one of those festivals I was standing at the gate entrance... waiting for the pizza lady to cross the street. In this case the pizza lady was Rosie Cerulla.... She was my Aunt Josie Delseno's sister and a very good friend of my mom. Anyway, as she made her way toward me with the large pan of pizza, she spotted two men about to enter the festival. These men were "merri-cons." This was a term used by the Italians, in our neighborhood, for non-local, non-Italian, people. It meant "Americans" in lieu of being Italian. Anyway, Rosie approached them and asked them if they wanted to buy some "la beesz." The men said, "buy what?" Rosie said "pizza, pizza pie." These two "merri-cons" looked at the pizza and then at each other with puzzled expressions. They had no idea what this was. One of them asked "What was on it, strawberries?" Rosie said, "no, that's tomatoes." Well, when these two guys heard her say tomatoes, they crinkled their noses in disgust and walked away.*

From left to right: Buddy LaRosa's Aunt Dena Panaro Minella and his grandmother, Josephine Palmire Panaro, who brought her family's recipes from Salerno, Italy. *Courtesy of the LaRosa Corporation.*

> *One of the ladies that helped make pizza in the church kitchen was Mrs. (Josephine Palmire) Panaro. In the mid 1950s her grandson, Donald "Buddy" Larosa, took this pizza idea and ran with it.*
>
> *From that small neighborhood, 15 other men, many related by blood or marriage, would go on to start their own pizzeria's.*

The first pizzeria to come out of the Little Italy neighborhood was Pasquale's, founded in 1953 at 1742 Queen City Avenue by Vinny and Pasquale (Pat) Gramaglia and their cousin, Lou Roberto. Pasquale's became the first chain pizza restaurant in the country. The Gramaglias' father, Vito, had emigrated from Modugno, Italy, in the Puglia region. He and his wife, Lilian, raised nine kids on a working-class machinist's salary. Pasquale had served in the navy during World War II as a cook on a submarine, where he developed his love for cooking. Vinny was a baker and developed the thin pizza crust. Lou would open the Newport, Kentucky location in 1957.

Pasquale's was also famous for bringing the stromboli to Cincinnati after its creation in 1950 in Philadelphia. The stromboli is named after a small island in the Tyrrhenian Sea, off the north coast of Sicily, containing one of the three active volcanoes in Italy.

The restaurant chaining began with the family. Pat wanted to open more stores, so one year later, he sold that first store to his sister Louise Bellisimo and his father, Vito Gramaglia, for $6,000 total. His Aunt Louise operated that store from 1954 to 1984. Pat's sister Marie Isadore owned the Colerain Avenue franchise, opened in 1959, which then became Isadore's pizza in 1978 when her son Joe Isadore took over.

That same year, Vinny and Pat's sister Cecilia Gramaglia and her husband, Jim DeCamp, moved to Indianapolis to open a location on Troy Avenue, eventually opening up three more locations that their sons helped to run. Another Gramaglia brother-in-law, Cliff Newman, with Pat's sister Tulie Newman, opened a Bridgetown franchise, and in 1962, it became the first franchisee of Empress Chili. Brothers Joe and Frank "Geech" Gramaglia helped out in the commissary. Still another Little Italy guy, Frank Baudendistle, opened another Pasquale's franchise.

Pat was friends with Len Goorian, producer of the *Uncle Al* and *Paul Gibson* shows locally. Len, along with Mike Tanguy, remodeled and rebranded the Queen City store and helped with promotion and advertising. Len was responsible for drawing the Pasquale's pizza guy mascot still used today. Pasquale's would advertise on the *Uncle Al Show*, along with Barq's Root Beer and Mama's Cookies, two other Cincinnati iconic brands. For every new grand opening, Uncle Al would emcee live on the radio for promotion.

Also helping the franchising was the fact that Vinny, a baker by trade, had developed a pizza dough that didn't need refrigeration. They also made the dough at a commissary and shipped to the franchise locations, saving franchisees startup costs of a dough mixer and large refrigeration.

The first commissary was Camp Washington, where they baked their own hoagie buns and made dough. Then they moved to a large four-floor former meatpacking plant at Massachusetts and Township. The first floor ran the catering business, and the second floor was their meat processing—pepperoni, sausage and other specialties. The third floor was the bakery, and the fourth floor was a frozen foods plant. The first frozen pizza sold in a Kroger grocery was a Pasquale's frozen pizza.

Networking, connections and a spirit of helpfulness were alive in the Cincinnati family business community during the 1950s and 1960s. The Gramaglia family knew Buddy LaRosa, the Lambrinides of Skyline and the Kiradjieffs of Empress—they all helped one another out and helped a lot of family and friends build livelihoods. The Gramaglias are actually related to the LaRosas by marriage.

The 125-location company was sold in 1966 to Neal Andrews, a Hyde Park franchisee and investors from Birmingham, Alabama. The Newport and Bellevue, Kentucky locations still operate locally. In 1986, Labatts Brewery needed a business in the United States for tax reasons and bought the company for a lot of money but let it go downhill. There are now only twelve Pasquale's stores.

Other men from Little Italy who started pizzerias included the Carotas, who started Beppo Pizza on Harrison Avenue; John Cipriani, who founded Cipriani's Pizza in Sayler Park; Andriacco's Pizza in North College Hill; Herman Minella, who had a pizza place in Mount Adam; and Mike Urti.

Another guy from Little Italy was closely watching the success of the Pasquale's Pizza business. Although not the first, LaRosa's Pizza is one Westside tradition that has stood the test of time and has become an icon for the entire city. Founded in 1954 by Cincinnati's Pizza King, Donald "Buddy" LaRosa, on Boudinot Avenue, it now has 35 percent market share of the Cincinnati pizza market, with sixty-four locations dotted around the city. About sixteen are corporate or family owned, and the remainder are franchises. Serving pizza, pasta, hoagies, calzones and other Italian-American fare, it offers more than forty menu items. It is the exclusive pizza sold at Kings Island Amusement Park, the Cincinnati Zoo, the Bengals' Paul Brown Stadium, the Reds' Great American Ballpark, Coney Island, Riverbend Music Center and the Nutter Center at the University of Dayton. In addition to more than $139 million of in-store revenue in 2013, LaRosa's also makes money from retail sales of its sauce, frozen garlic bread, meatballs and salad dressing. Its sales equate to more than 6.5 million pizzas per year.

Originally called Papa Gino's, Buddy and Soldano soon bought out their two other buddies from the neighborhood: his cousin, Richard "Mussie" Minella, and Frank "Head" Serraino. Then Buddy bought out Soldano, who wanted to branch out with more stores, while he just wanted to make a living. He renamed the pizza stand LaRosa's in 1960 when the business really took off, and in 1961, he opened his first sit-down restaurant, the Italian Inn, on Boudinot. He bought more property nearby and opened LaRosa's Wine

A view of the original LaRosa's Pizza on Boudinot Avenue as it looked in the 1960s. *Courtesy of the LaRosa Corporation.*

Cellar and Italian Market. These made up LaRosa's "Italian Village," which mimicked a similar concept Buddy had seen in Chicago.

Mike Soldano would keep the Papa Gino's name and open up his own pizza parlor at Harrison Avenue and Race Road in Bridgetown, which he operated until 1981.

Donald Sebastiano LaRosa grew up on Queen City Avenue in South Fairmount's "Little Italy" during the Great Depression. LaRosa's parents divorced when he was five, and he grew up in his grandmother's house, surrounded by uncles who nicknamed him "Buddy." At the mostly German St. Bonaventure, Buddy was taunted for being Italian. In defiance, he slicked his hair back with olive oil, displaying his Italian pride. His parents wanted

An ad for LaRosa's shows the murals created by William Hemsath in the original Boudinot store. *Courtesy of the Price Hill Historical Society.*

The original logo, Luigi, was drawn for Buddy by an art teacher from Western Hills High.
Courtesy of the Price Hill Historical Society.

him to attend a Franciscan-run high school, like their local parish church. So Buddy woke up at 6:00 a.m. to take three bus transfers east to St. Bernard to attend Roger Bacon High School. He graduated in 1948 with the goal, as his senior yearbook states, "to own the largest fruit store in the country" and joined the navy.

The signature sweet sauce is the recipe of Buddy's maternal aunt, Magdalena "Dena" Panaro Minella. Naples has long been considered the birthplace of pizza, originally a peasant food. And although the Panaro family was from Naples, the marinara sauce originated with Dena's mother, Josephine Palmire Panaro, whose family came from Salerno, one bay down the "boot" toward the Amalfi Coast from Naples. Salerno is the area where the sweet and rich San Marzano tomato is cultivated. This plum tomato is prized by chefs worldwide for its sweetness, lower acidity than Roma tomatoes and deep flavor, and it is the reason LaRosa's sauce is so sweet.

After returning to Cincinnati in 1953, Buddy helped his mother, Maria, and Aunt Dena make and serve their pizzas for fifteen cents per square at the church summer festival. He saw how popular pizza was at home, too, and decided that this was where he was going to make his living. His own Sicilian-born father, Antonio LaRosa, called him crazy for trying pizza, especially in a predominantly German/Irish city. From owning his own wholesale produce business on Elder Street that serviced Findlay Market, Antonio noted, "Cincinnatians eat potatoes, not pizza."

Ignoring the naysayers, Buddy believed that he was opening into a rising market. Pizza was ready to boom, fueled by the appetites of teenagers. To them, pizza was the hip new food of teen rebellion. Buddy used this fact and became the first guerrilla marketeer, bringing pizza to football practices and inviting students to the pizzeria for spaghetti dinners, hoping that they'd come back and bring their friends.

In the early 1980s, LaRosa's began home and business delivery but with its full menu of items, unlike other competitors. In 1991, it launched the "one-number" call center at 513-347-1111 and, in 2003, launched online ordering. On July 14, 1991, Scott "Big Dog" Steidel went to the original location on Boudinot and demanded a meeting with Buddy to personally thank him for everything he had done for Lower Price Hill over the years. Buddy was so touched by the gesture that he rewarded Scott with a week's worth of free pizza and said, "Thanks for being my buddy." This gave LaRosa's the idea for the Buddy Card, which has been its loyalty program since then and has supported literally thousands of teams and organizations.

It also was a way to build its business against the national chains during the competitive "Pizza Wars" of the '90s.

After building a successful venture on the Westside, buddy's first franchisee in 1967 was his hoagie supplier, Ed Eilers. Seeing how much he was delivering to the Boudinot store, Eilers convinced Buddy to let him open a LaRosa's on Winton and Galbraith in Finneytown. More franchises followed in Clifton, White Oak and Hyde Park, and franchising really picked up steam in the 1970s. By 1980, there were twenty-five restaurants and fifty-five by 2004.

At eighty-three, Buddy is not ready to hang up his apron. Even though he is essentially retired from operations—his son Mike is CEO, son Mark is president and grandson Nick is involved in new franchising agreements—he wants to see expansion into Columbus and Tennessee before taking his hands fully out of the marinara sauce.

The differences between Pasquale's and LaRosa's can be boiled down into carryout versus full-service restaurants. As far as taste, LaRosa's sauce is sweet, while Pasquale's is more tart, with an oregano blast. Pasquale's had franchised to 125 restaurants in 1966, before LaRosa's began franchising largely. When the new Pasquale's owners focused on the South, it gave Buddy a chance to win the franchising war and a larger share of the pizza market.

Other pizzerias began popping up in the late 1950s in Greater Cincinnati as the pizza revolution ignited. In 1956, Bert Georgiton, an immigrant from southern Greece, opened Papa Dino's Pizza on Calhoun Street in Clifton, remembered fondly by generations of University of Cincinnati students.

John Byington opened Silverton Pizza in 1957 on Montgomery Road. It then moved to a larger location on Plainfield Road, changing its name to Italianette Pizza, and is still in operation under the management of Fritz and Shirley Kimmer.

Al Jones, who started working for Pasquale's, founded Angilo's pizza in 1958 at Jefferson Avenue in Reading, which is still operating in Cincinnati. By 1968, Angilo's boasted forty locations and the need to move into a larger commissary.

The steam of LaRosa's franchising boom in the 1970s saw others wanting a piece of the pizza pie. Germantown Pizza, started in the early 1970s, boasted locations in North College Hill, St. Bernard, Mount Washington, Sharonville, Western Hills, Northside, Oakley and Swifton Center. Richard and Donna Walsh opened Germantown Pizza on Vine Street in St. Bernard in 1973, which ran into the 1990s as a pre- and post-game eatery for generations of Roger Bacon students. Kathy Engelhardt and her former husband opened the North College Hill location in 1976 and operated it until 1989. They offered a breakfast menu, pizza, hoagies, cheesecake and neighborhood gossip. Germantown's pizza was thin crust, had a sweet sauce that was more brown than red, had good sausage and used round-cut onions that were crispy when cooked. They were also known for their hoagies.

In 1975, Ray Spurlock founded Mio's Pizza on Paxton Avenue in Hyde Park. Mio's pioneered home delivery in 1980, was the first local pizzeria to use conveyor ovens and was one of the first to introduce the deep-dish pizza. The year 1976 saw Gramma's Pizza in Mount Carmel open, which now has six locations on the far east side of Cincinnati. Finally, in 1978, Robert Rotunda of Fort Mitchell, Kentucky, founded the Snappy Tomato Pizza, which still has many locations throughout Cincinnati. During the cicada emergence of 1987, it created a jingle making Cincinnatians think that it offered a cicada pizza. After only a ten-year run, local Spooner's Pizza, founded in 1985 by Michael Bauer, sold its locations to Snappy's in 1994.

Habig's: Comfort at the Crossroads

From 1933 to 2004, Habig's Family Restaurant at 3081 Harrison Avenue and Epworth Avenue in Westwood served home-style German food. It served local favorites like barley and mock turtle soup, sauerbraten, baked liver pudding, grilled knockwurst, grilled smoked hot mett and, of course, hot bacon slaw.

Habig's was owned and operated by three generations of the same family. Founder Henry Habig Sr. and his wife, Sophie, were the first to run it. Next came their son, Henry Jr. It was recently run by four of Henry's sons: Duane and Chris Habig in the front of the house and Mark and Jay in the kitchen.

One of the specialties was Sophie Habig's Concord grape pie. Many loyal customers say it was the best reason to go there. Made with Concord grapes that were only available in the fall, the family hired extra help to process the grapes to be frozen so that the pie could be available all year round. The resulting pie is a bright purple with a naturally thickened filling and powdered sugar–dusted crust. The flavor brings up memories of a grape arbor in September.

Left: A menu cover from Habig's promotes its 1933 roots. *Courtesy of the Public Library of Cincinnati and Hamilton County.*

Below: Habig's vintage neon sign, showing a gentle pour of the martini glass, is now on display at the American Sign Museum. *Courtesy of American Sign Museum.*

Cincinnati Sauerbraten

1 rump roast
vinegar
2 large onions cut in half
salt and pepper
2 teaspoons pickling spices in a bag
flour
granulated sugar
gingersnaps
lemon juice

In a pot cover raw rump with ratio of half a part vinegar and two-thirds of a part water. Add 2 large onions cut in half, salt and pepper and the pickling spices in a bag. Cover and marinate in the refrigerator from 1 to 3 days, depending on cut of meat. Put in cooking pot and cook for 1 hour. Dry brown about ½ cup of flour and add to pot with about ½ cup sugar, a handful of crumbled gingersnaps and several dashes of lemon juice. Cook another 2 hours.

Cincinnati German Hot Slaw

5 slices of bacon
head of small cabbage, shredded
1½ tablespoons sugar
dash of salt and black pepper
1 small onion, chopped
2½ tablespoons apple cider vinegar

Add the fried, crumbled bacon to cabbage, which has been mixed with sugar, salt and pepper and onion. Cover and let stand. When ready to serve, add vinegar to bacon grease left in pan and reheat. Pour hot over cabbage and serve immediately.

Directly next to Habig's was the Window Garden, which opened in 1937 and remained open until 2000. Like Habig's, it also served the German sauerbraten with red cabbage and American home-style items like roast turkey, filet of fish and beef Wellington. Although it served similar items, the Window Garden had more depth in its menu than Habig's.

A 1960s ad for the Window Garden. *Courtesy of the Price Hill Historical Society.*

Sarah Felix started the Window Garden as a tearoom in order to send her son to college. Although the restaurant still retained its traditional theme, David Pavlik added contemporary food to complement the home-style seafood pasta with roasted garlic and a dinner salad with field greens, gorgonzola cheese and pine nuts, something Ms. Felix would not have recognized.

Pavlik, owner of the Window Garden for twenty-five years, said that the stability of the Westwood community, where people have a respect for tradition, helped his business. People patronized it *and* its friendly competitor next door because they were places that had always been there. There is a bit of a suspicion of new things on the Westside.

THE TINIEST COVE IN CHEVIOT

Another old-timer in the heart of Cheviot, nine blocks away from Habig's, is Maury's Tiny Cove, which has been serving meat, potatoes and martinis since 1949. Opened by Maurice "Maury" Bibent IV, the son of French immigrant parents, the restaurant was anything but French. He operated it until he retired and sold to brothers Paul and Ben Yamaguchi in 1994, who sold to Mike Huesmann in 2010.

Maury purchased Tolles Tiny Cove in 1949. Back then, the Cove was a small one-room bar. Bibent purchased the two adjacent buildings and expanded the premises into what would become the Westside's oldest family steakhouse. Maury served steaks, seafood and chicken dishes to friends and neighbors, who from the 1950s to the 1970s would line up outside the door to eat at the hot spot.

Maury's passion for sports inspired him to do an ingenious thing. He named his steaks after local teams. The Musketeer, named after St. Xavier University's mascot, was the chopped sirloin. The Bomber, St. Xavier High School's mascot, was the name for the prime rib. The Bearcat was the name for the filet mignon. Purcell Marian High School's mascot, the Cavalier, became the name for the strip sirloin steak, and the Bengal became the finest top sirloin steak for two. The Panther, Elder High School's mascot, was the name for the cod sandwich.

The Cove became a popular pregame eatery for Westsiders. For many, it still is, as well as a place for prom and Father-Daughter Dances at Seton and Mother of Mercy High Schools.

Stepping into the restaurant is like stepping back in time. Its low-hanging ceiling, wood-paneled walls and red booths, flanked with mirrors, evoke the 1950s. During a sixty-fifth anniversary celebration, Huesmann auctioned off some of original owner Maury's bulls to complete renovations to lighten and update the place out of the mid-twentieth century. Maury was a Taurus and collected bulls in all his

Maury's Tiny Cove sign, with its martini-toting bull, beckons visitors in. *Author's collection.*

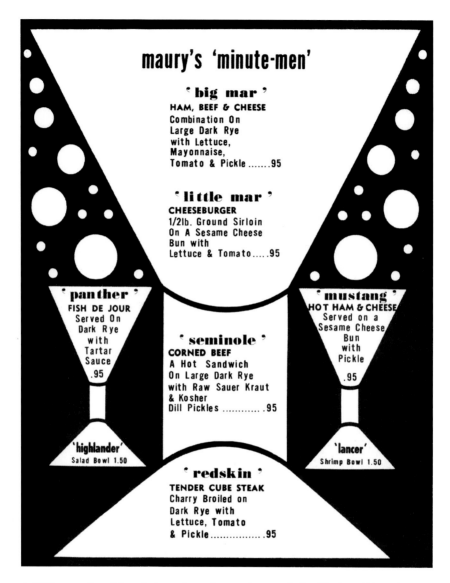

A 1950s menu from Maury's shows the various steaks named after Cincinnati high school and college sports teams. *Courtesy of the Public Library of Cincinnati and Hamilton County.*

travels, displaying them throughout the restaurant. He even used a martini-drinking steer as the restaurant mascot.

Huesmann keeps the same steak names but has butchers on site to keep prices low to compete against other steakhouses popping up in the neighborhood and keep the now sixty-six-year Westside tradition going.

A Stone's Throw Away

Stone's family restaurant on Harrison in between Habig's and Maury's serves goetta and eggs, pot roast and meatloaf. It was one of the very few restaurants in Cincinnati where you could order another local dish: city chicken. It also serves its own version of Cincinnati-style chili. Opened in 1962 by Mike and Mary Topalis Stone, their daughter, Stephanie, now does all the cooking. She still makes baklava from her Greek mother's recipe.

Santorini

This hidden gem on the Westside has been owned by the Dinez family for more than thirty years. Santorini Restaurant on Harrison in Cheviot is typical of a Greek diner, serving standard gyros, spanakopita, baklava and Cincinnati-style chili, along with double-deckers, hamburgers, steak and breakfast all day. Surrounded by pictures of the Greek island of Santorini and other Greek islands, it certainly makes you want to call a travel agent after dinner.

Sebastian's

Sebastian's on Glenway Avenue in Western Hills was founded in 1976 by Alex Vassiliou, a Greek immigrant from a village near Kastoria, Greece, the same area from where the Lambrinides of Skyline Chili emigrated. Alex spent time in Sweden and Germany working for a fur manufacturer before deciding to settle in America. First coming to Chicago, he didn't like the big city and decided to come to Cincinnati, where he had cousins.

Buddy LaRosa helped Alex get the restaurant off the ground, and in honor of him, Alex named the restaurant Sebastian's, Buddy's middle name. With his family, Alex has worked hard to keep this restaurant open for nearly forty years. Alex's daughter, Helen, and wife, Sue, work alongside him in the kitchen.

Considered by many to have the best gyro in town, Sebastian's is a small luncheonette with a counter and several booths. It sells enough gyros to have three spits of gyro meat rotating in the kitchen. In addition to its famous

Sebastian's beckons diners in for the best gyro in town at its corner location on Glenway Avenue. *Author's collection.*

gyros, the menu has other Greek specialties like domathakia (grape leaves stuffed with rice and ground beef), spanakopita and tiropita (spinach- and cheese-filled pastries).

LAKE NINA

A bit farther out in the Westside, just off Pippin Road on the shores of the small lake, is Lake Nina Restaurant & Tavern. The lodge-like building is nestled behind a strip of stores and in front of the small lake that lends its name. It has been around since the mid-1950s. A bit eclectic and a bit old school, there's definitely something special about Lake Nina. It's a family place with placemats instead of tablecloths, bright lights, TV and pinball machines in the background. You know you're on the Westside when you see hot slaw, chicken liver and mock turtle soup on the menu. It is famous for its fish log, a large boneless Icelandic piece of cod that becomes a must-have during Lent. In addition, it has fried chicken, double-deckers and Cincinnati-style chili. Cheese coneys are not on the menu but can be requested off menu.

TAKE THE TROLLEY t
a land of find food an
fun. Come to a worl
highlighted by dinner
and delicacies. Wher
tantalizing aromas per
meate the air and sea
foods are a specialty.

Trolley Tavern
4332 River Rd.

A 1963 ad for the Trolley Tavern shows a West High school student enjoying an after-school meal. *Courtesy of the Price Hill Historical Society.*

Trolley Tavern

The Trolley Tavern location at Anderson Ferry and River Road opened in the early 1900s as a popular stop on the other side of the Anderson Ferry and at the end of an interurban trolley line. During its heyday under owner Al Lederle, it was known as the "Cricket of the Westside."

Known as Captain Al's, it was a log cabin until the 1937 flood washed it away. Then owner Al Lederle brought in two trolley cars, built a space between them and just kept adding on. A reproduction trolley car was built in the front in 1972 and then a back dining room seating 250, a ballroom seating 400 and the upstairs Flying Bridge for private parties up to 125.

The specialty of the Trolley Tavern was seafood, namely its "jack salmon," which was either pike or pickerel. The filet was served deep-fried and succulent, and a whole jack salmon entrée was deboned at the table and served with lemon and tartar sauce. Numerous other beef, pork and seafood choices filled the menu. All dinners came with potatoes and a salad, one of which might be hot slaw, which was a favorite. For dessert, its turtle pie was also a big seller.

Chapter 9
BELOVED BRANDS

Cincinnati has many beloved food brands that have reached national renown. Some have gone to food heaven but still exist as strong food memories for those who enjoyed them. Others you can still find being served alongside a sandwich at a local restaurant, next to an egg sunnyside up or just in a bowl with a spoon.

GOETTA A' GO-GO

Mention goetta anywhere other than Cincinnati and you'll get puzzled looks. But mention it in Cincinnati and you'll get a monologue on what meat market has the best, how it's best prepared and what condiment you should use to dress it. Only in Cincinnati do we know about such things. Goetta is a breakfast food of the German immigrants.

Goetta has become so embedded in Cincinnati culture that it's reached pop icon status. Goetta is a lifestyle. It allows us to eat back to our immigrant ancestry or chomp back in time. It allows us to accept and celebrate our own German peasant provinciality. There are not one but two Goettafests held yearly. Like a second Civil War, many families in Greater Cincinnati stand divided as to whether it should be prepared crispy or mushy or if it should be served with ketchup, grape jelly or syrup.

Celebrities and public figures have chimed in about goetta. It had reached such national exposure that President George W. Bush asked in 2006, "What *is* goetta?" How we define it today has always been tricky. It's easiest to describe its ingredients. Originally a breakfast food, it's a high-energy combination of pork, beef, pinhead oats, onions and one of two spice blends. It looks like a sausage and has a consistency similar to a meatloaf, but it's not dense enough to be either.

In Germany, goetta's ancestors were referred to under the umbrella of *gruetzwurst*, or grain sausages, often made at the time of pig slaughter with the scraps left over from the pig or animal. Today, most goetta recipes do not use organ meats.

Brought over by north German immigrants from Westphalia, North Saxony, Hanover and Mecklenburg to Cincinnati around the 1840s, goetta has been a part of Cincinnati food culture ever since. It was originally an economical food meant to extend small amounts of expensive meat like pork and beef, a way to extend the lesser cuts of pork like organ and head meat and a way to extend shelf life of meat before refrigeration. With Cincinnati's pork packing history, there has always been a supply of inexpensive pork in the city, so goetta evolved into less of a slaughter sausage and more of a quality meat grain sausage.

The goetta you would have eaten in an Over-the-Rhine tenement house in the 1850s would not be the same as what you would eat today at Frisch's. The early forms from north European gruetzwursts were much more like porridges than terrines. And they were descended from the blood sausages or black puddings of Teutonic Europe, like haggis. Some forms of the German gruetzwursts still contain blood in them. Modern forms still present today in Germany are knipp, pinkel and panhas. They vary in the type of grain, type of meat and spice blend. Knipp is from the Hanover region, made with oat groats and pork organs and spiced with salt, pepper and allspice. It's served on whole grain bread with boiled potatoes, pickles, apple sauce, sweet and sour pumpkin or even beet root. Pinkel is from Bremen, Oldenburg, Osnabruck and Frisia and is made with bacon, oat groats or barley and pork. It's eaten with kale. Panhas is made with pork parts and buckwheat in the north or pearl barley in the south.

An old family goetta recipe's origin can be traced by its spice blend. There are two schools of spice when it comes to goetta. There's the more standard pepper, cloves and allspice. And then there's the other more herby version, using sage, rosemary, marjoram, summer savory or a combination thereof. Both versions also contain bay leaf. The standard spice blend is similar to most north German sausages and traces back to Hanover, Oldenburg, Westphalia and Mecklenburg immigrants. The second blend comes from southern German immigrants or Anglo immigrants who used the herby spice blend for meat stuffings.

These various regional types of gruetzwurst gave rise to different forms when German immigrants came to America. Scrapple is a descendant of panhas and eaten in Maryland, Pennsylvania and Delmarva Peninsula. Scrapple uses cornmeal instead of pinhead oats and also uses pork organ meat. Livermush is the version of scrapple eaten in the Carolinas, also called pork pudding in South Carolina. Pruttles is the version of goetta that Volga German Americans in central Kansas eat. The only difference between it and goetta is that it uses rolled oat groats (the whole oat, with the husk, or bran, left removed) instead of pinhead oats (oats cut in slices with the husk intact). There isn't really a noticeable texture difference between rolled oats and steel cut or pinhead oats, but when you cook each, only the pinhead oats in goetta will occasionally "pop" out of their husks, like mini-popcorn. It's nature's own thermometer to alarm you when the pan heat is too high for goetta.

Outside of the Greater Cincinnati "Goetta Perimeter," German Americans in southeast Indiana and north-central and northwest Ohio call it grits or German grits, not to be confused with the southern hominy grits. And the Amish communities still call their version, which uses cornmeal, panhas. Even boudin, the sausage native to Louisiana and the bayou, can be considered like these others a grain sausage, as its filler is rice.

Today in Cincinnati, there are more than one hundred restaurants that serve goetta. Izzy's has a goetta reuben. The Rookwood Pottery has a goetta hanky panky appetizer. Many local pizzerias have goetta pizzas. There are goetta link cheese coneys, deep-fried goetta balls, goetta eggs Benedict, goetta hot browns, goetta corn dogs, goetta nachos and even a goetta/apricot Danish.

THE GOETTA FAMILY TREE

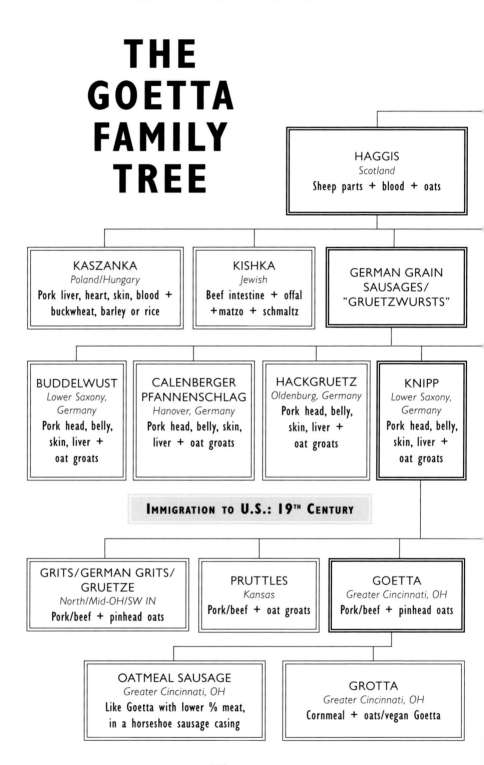

HAGGIS
Scotland
Sheep parts + blood + oats

KASZANKA
Poland/Hungary
Pork liver, heart, skin, blood + buckwheat, barley or rice

KISHKA
Jewish
Beef intestine + offal +matzo + schmaltz

GERMAN GRAIN SAUSAGES/ "GRUETZWURSTS"

BUDDELWUST
Lower Saxony, Germany
Pork head, belly, skin, liver + oat groats

CALENBERGER PFANNENSCHLAG
Hanover, Germany
Pork head, belly, skin, liver + oat groats

HACKGRUETZ
Oldenburg, Germany
Pork head, belly, skin, liver + oat groats

KNIPP
Lower Saxony, Germany
Pork head, belly, skin, liver + oat groats

IMMIGRATION TO U.S.: 19TH CENTURY

GRITS/GERMAN GRITS/ GRUETZE
North/Mid-OH/SW IN
Pork/beef + pinhead oats

PRUTTLES
Kansas
Pork/beef + oat groats

GOETTA
Greater Cincinnati, OH
Pork/beef + pinhead oats

OATMEAL SAUSAGE
Greater Cincinnati, OH
Like Goetta with lower % meat, in a horseshoe sausage casing

GROTTA
Greater Cincinnati, OH
Cornmeal + oats/vegan Goetta

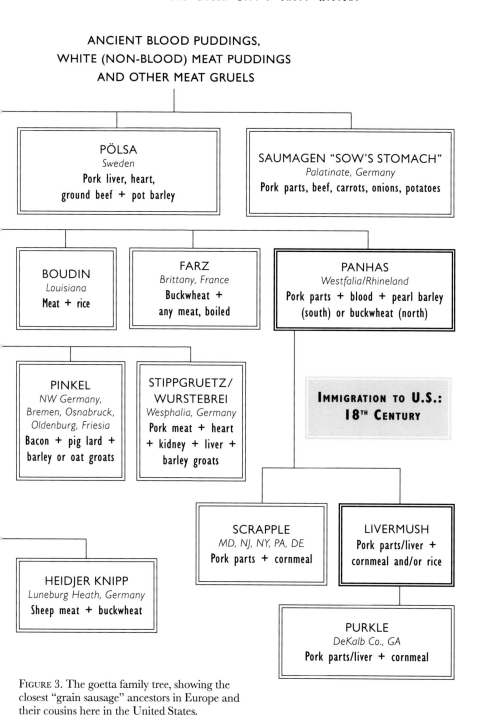

FIGURE 3. The goetta family tree, showing the closest "grain sausage" ancestors in Europe and their cousins here in the United States.

Dorsel's Goetta

6 cups water

3 teaspoons salt

pinch of pepper

2½ cups pinhead oatmeal

1 pound ground beef

1 pound ground pork

1 large onion, sliced

1 to 4 bay leaves

Put water, salt and pepper into crockpot. Cover and heat on high 20 minutes. Add oatmeal, cover and cook on high 1½ hours. Add meat, onion and bay leaves. Mix well and then cover and cook on low for 3 hours. Uncover; if not thick enough, cook longer, stirring often. Pour into bread pans. Cool and refrigerate. Slice the loaf of goetta and fry slices crispy in a pan of bacon fat. Serve with ketchup, jelly or maple syrup.

ECKERLIN'S BEST GOETTA

One of the oldest goetta brands in Cincinnati is Eckerlin Meats. The founder, Ernie Eckerlin, a German immigrant from Baden, first opened a slaughterhouse in Cincinnati in 1852. Then, when Findlay Market opened in 1855, he set up his daughter, Frieda, at a retail stand, where they sold samples of Ernie's goetta recipe. Frieda married an employee, Al Lillis, and their son, Bob Lillis, operated their stand at Findlay Market until passing it on to the fifth generation, Bob Jr.

Bob makes "Eckerlin's Best Goetta" daily from the family recipe, which is more than one hundred years old. Eckerlin's uses only high-quality beef and pork in its goetta, with no scraps or excess fat added. It's stirred every twelve minutes as it slow cooks for four hours. On the label is a turn-of-the-last-century photograph of his grandmother Frieda's brother Adolph Ecklerin's butcher shop in Mount Adams. The sign below the counter reads, "The best goetta in town." Bob ships their goetta all over the United States, and it has been voted Best Goetta in Cincinnati three times by *Cincinnati* magazine. They sell more than five hundred pounds of it a week, or twenty-six thousand pounds a year, to Cincinnatians who cast their vote with their wallet.

Gotta Get Some Glier's

Glier's may not be the oldest producer, but it is by far the largest producer of goetta in Greater Cincinnati. Produced in an old Bavarian Brewery factory in the Lewisburg neighborhood of Covington, Kentucky, Glier's holds more than 90 percent of the goetta market, producing more than 1 million pounds of goetta per year.

The company was founded in 1946 by Bob Glier upon his return from World War II, with help from his mother, Emma Ann Yung, whose family had a butcher shop and dairy in Covington on Madison Avenue. His mother's goetta recipe was more of a porridge, with only about 20 percent meat, that was held in crocks and stood up without refrigeration for about a week. Bob experimented with texture by adding more meat and made the goetta more substantial. He started with a small retail shop at 439 Pike Street in Covington, Kentucky. In the 1950s, Bob saw the future in just goetta, and he and his wife, Louise, gave up the retail shop for a factory.

By the 1960s, the United States Department of Agriculture saw that it was necessary to create standards for local meat products like goetta, so it used Glier's as the national standard for goetta, which requires 50 percent meat or meat byproducts. It was the first company to make a goetta in a shrink-wrapped package that held up on shelves. Before refrigeration, goetta was only eaten between Labor Day and Memorial Day. Glier's uses pork hearts and skin in its goetta recipe, which gives it its color and texture.

Now operated by Bob's son, Dan Glier, the company today employs twenty-five people at the factory. Its largest customer is Kroger's, but it also sells to Walmart, as well as local restaurants like Frisch's and Perkins. Its largest competitor in the goetta market is Queen City sausage.

A casing of Glier's spicy goetta, the next generation of Cincinnati goetta. *Author's collection.*

Glier's is also responsible for changing the pronunciation of goetta. Originally and correctly pronounced "gutt-a," with its umlauted *o*, Dan thought it sounded too close to "guts," which he didn't want associated with goetta. There was a local jeweler in Covington called Goetz that pronounced its name "getz," and Dan used it as an example of how goetta should be pronounced.

Glier's also manufactures a spicy version, a lower-fat turkey version and goetta sausage links. It also sponsors Goettafest, which in 2014 saw more than 200,000 people from thirty-seven countries and fifty states.

Rubel's Rye Bread

In Cincinnati, one can't mention rye bread without recalling the beloved brand Rubel's Heidelberg Rye Bread. Generations of Cincinnatians sandwiched their braunschweiger, their stinky Limburger cheese and onions or their reuben sandwiches with Rubel's rye bread. And we have founder and Russian Jewish immigrant Elias F. Rubel to thank for this legacy. Elias founded the Rubel Baking Company in 1882. Originally at 570–74 West Sixth Street, the company grew with his five sons, all of whom worked with him at the bakery.

Three of Rubel's sons—Ben, Max and Sam—took over the business and constructed the new factory in 1930 at the corner of Melish and Bathgate in the Avondale neighborhood. At that time, it was one of the largest baking plants in the country, and it had an open house on Tuesday, July 22, 1930, to show it off.

Many hundreds of Cincinnati schoolchildren have toured the plant on class field trips, remembering the smell of the fresh bread baking in the ovens.

Rubel's was most famous for the Heidelberg rye bread, which was the first sliced, cellophane-wrapped bread in Cincinnati when it was introduced in 1933. But it also manufactured milk bread, Vienna bread (with poppyseed), Kimmel rye, pumpernickel, whole wheat, rolls and pastries. The bread would come with cornflakes at the bottom for ease in transport over the conveyor belts and packaging equipment. But to many, that made it seem even more handmade.

It had a great presence in print advertising in the local newspapers with cartoons and ads. Its slogan, "Hearth Baked on Stone," was synonymous with its Rubel brand, and it had a catchy radio jingle. In the 1940s, it even sponsored a radio show called *Fans in the Stands*, hosted pregame at the Reds' Crosley Field by Dick Bray. Bray would interview both kids and adults, and everyone interviewed would get a photo and a coupon for a free loaf of Rubel's bread.

The company remained in business until March 1978, nearly one hundred years, when Pennington Breads in Norwood, Ohio, bought the formulas and trade names for Rubel's breads. Walter Rubel, company president and grandson of the founder, was the last member of the family participating in the company's operation.

Off with Their Heads, but Leave Their Opera Cream!

The opera cream is a candy uniquely Cincinnati, brought here by a German confection-making family before the Civil War. It's an oblong chocolate, sometimes mistaken for the round butter cream, with a rich filling of sweet cream, sugar and butter. The opera cream has a legacy dating all the way back to the French empire of the 1600s and the extravagant "Sun King," Louis XIV. The opera creams that we love are the same recipe that Louis XIV ate in his gilded palace as his imperial subjects starved in the streets.

It all started back in 1668. A German chocolate confection family, the Bissingers, were living in Paris. That year, King Louis XIV proclaimed the family "Confiseur Imperial," or candy makers of the empire, because their candies were his favorite. The Bissinger fame began to spread, and the family continued to make confections for the royals and nobles of Europe.

The Bissingers continued making their chocolates for the French after the French Revolution, acting as confiseur to Emperor Louis-Napoleon Bonaparte III. Legend has it that Napoleon Bonaparte I carried chocolate morsels into his military campaigns in the nineteenth century, eating them to conserve energy—in a sense inventing the first power bars.

The Bissingers, led by Karl Friedrich Bissinger (1829–1905), left Europe in 1845 to escape the rising turmoil and dissatisfaction with the French king Louis Philippe and settled in Cincinnati, continuing to make candies here. With them they brought their delicious opera cream recipe. Legend has it that they supplied these opera cream candies to the Cincinnati Opera at the Music Hall, where operagoers received them free at intermission. After Karl Sr. died, his widow, Theresa, became the first female owner of a chocolate company in the United States. Karl Jr. decided to move to St. Louis. He opened the store there in 1927, where it remains in business today.

Several other companies in Cincinnati started making the opera cream as its popularity spread throughout the area. Putnam Candies on Central Avenue took on the Bissinger recipe. Putnam was then bought by Chris A. Papas and Sons in 1967. Papas Candies was run by a Greek family, starting in 1935 as Lilly's Candy Shop at Madison Avenue and Ninth Street in Covington, Kentucky. Bob Schneider, second-generation owner of Schneider's Candies in Dayton, Kentucky, worked at Papas Candies, learning its recipes. He then worked at and purchased Bissinger's, where he learned the original opera cream recipe. Bob took this recipe to his family's Sweet Shop in Dayton, Kentucky, where they continue to make this legacy recipe that survived the French Revolution.

Nearly One Hundred Years of Crunchy Goodness

Most big cities have their local potato chip company that's venerated above all others. In Cincinnati, we have two: Grippo's and Husman's, both founded in 1919.

Angelo Grippo started the Grippo Cone Company from a one-room office on West Court Street. Originally making rolled sugar cones, it wasn't until 1959 that it added potato chips. It stopped making the sugar cones in 1950. Grippo's added pretzels to its business and in 1923 began hand twisting and baking the traditional twist pretzels. The standard-sized pretzel sold for a penny each at retail locations throughout Greater Cincinnati.

In 1930, Angelo Grippo invented the "loop pretzel." Mr. Grippo wanted a simple pretzel that could be made easily and would resist breakage. The loop pretzel looks like a teardrop. Mr. Grippo not only invented but also constructed and put the pretzel-looping machines into operation.

Grippo's produces a full line of potato chips, flavored popcorn, tortilla chips, corn chips, fried cheese curls, cheese nips and salsa and onion dips. The barbecue chips, with the grilling chef logo, are the top seller, with a unique spice blend that's also bottled and sold in the retail grocers as a meat and salad marinade. Its other chip flavors are hot dill pickle, sweet Bermuda onion and cheese and jalapeño. You cannot get plain chips from Grippo's.

The classic Grippo's barbecue flavor has been a Cincinnati staple since about 1959. *Author's collection.*

The barbecue flavor starts as a texture. The soft crystalline flavor dust that completely coats the chip like a sugar cookie first coats your tongue. As the flavor dust dissolves, it creates a rush of sweetness, immediately followed by a vinegar-tinged heat that spreads over the tongue, across the palate and finally over the back of the throat. There is a faint salty taste and an earthy potato taste that accompany the stronger flavors.

Grippo's became one of the city's earliest female-run businesses when Angelo's wife, Emma, took over after his death and ran it to the 1970s, when her daughter, Dorothy Pagel, became the woman in charge. Now into the family's third generation, the "Fun Food Company" is run by five grandchildren of Angelo and Emma.

The plant in Colerain Township employs sixty workers and twenty more in local distribution. It has turned down offers from outside companies, and although Lay's has the majority of the local chip market, its products have a cult-like following, with Cincinnati expatriates ordering their childhood chips by mail order. It even offers free shipping to American soldiers overseas.

So strong is its cult following that local restaurants have added the barbecue flavor to their menus. Tom + Chee, the native Cincinnati grilled cheese sandwich chain, has added a Grippo Barbecue Chip Grilled Cheese to its sandwich lineup. The Incline Public House in Price Hill has a macaroni and cheese dish with crumbled Grippo's on top. The Senate Pub, a fancy hot dog bar in fashionable Gateway Corridor District, had the Trailer Park Dog, made with bacon, slaw, American cheese and crumbled Grippo's barbecue chips. The Rookwood has Grippo's Fries, skinny fries heavily seasoned with Grippo's barbecue seasoning, as well as Grippo's barbecue pork cracklings. Jenco Brothers Candy in Clifton sprinkles Grippo's seasoning on its white cheddar or regular cheddar popcorn and even makes a mix of Grippo's and caramel corn.

Harry Husman was a young twenty-four-year-old when he started the Husman Potato Products Company. As a paper bag salesman to grocers, he noticed customers always asking clerks for potato chips. As they were all made out of town, Husman saw an opportunity. His first plant was on the second floor of a building, so he had to hoist up sacks of potatoes by rope and pulley. The company is now owned by Agrilink Foods and makes five different types of potato chips—wavy, regular, sour cream and onion, wavy cheddar cheese and wavy hot barbecue. It also makes cheese corn and tortilla chips.

Frank's RedHot

Frank's RedHot is one of the most well-known and most used hot sauce brands in the United States. And it all started in Cincinnati as a leading product of the Frank Tea & Spice Company.

In 1918, Jacob Frank went to Louisiana to learn the pepper business and to find makers of a hot sauce based on cayenne pepper, different from the other familiar hot sauce at the time, Tabasco sauce, which was based on the tabasco pepper.

He partnered with Adam Estilette, from a Cajun farming family. Together they set up a pickling plant in New Iberia, Louisiana, to process the cayenne peppers they grew. The processed peppers would then be shipped to Cincinnati for further blending with other pure ingredients like salt, spices, garlic and vinegar and then aged in oak casks. In 1920, the first bottle of Frank's RedHot came out of this arrangement. After Adam's death, his sons, Frady and Grady, took over the reins for the Franks.

Frank's RedHot has another accolade in its history. It was the secret ingredient for the first-ever Buffalo wings, made by Teressa Bellissimo at the Anchor Bar and Grill in Buffalo, New York, in 1964.

Frank's
RED HOT SAUCE

For piquancy and flavor there is nothing quite like Frank's Red Hot Sauce. The secret of this famous sauce is in its special formula inspired by the spirited flavor of the foods served in the early days of New Orleans. In that unique city of America, so proud of its old world traditions of gracious living, there are cherished ways of creating sauces and flavors that have made New Orleans renowned for its culinary triumphs. Out of this heritage, Frank's Red Hot

Sauce was created. From the plantations of southern Louisiana, special peppers are selected, then cured and processed in the Frank New Iberia, Louisiana, plant. Shipped to Cincinnati, further blending with other pure ingredients, and processing and aging in oaken casks, complete the product which gives such new, delightful zest to meals. Marketed in popular sizes, Frank's Red Hot Sauce is the outstanding product of its kind.

An ad for Frank's RedHot that shows the connection to Louisiana, where it had a plant in New Iberia. *Courtesy of John Frank.*

Frank's was sold in 1969, and its Frank's RedHot brand was sold in 1977 to Durkee Famous Foods. Then, in 1995, Reckitt Benckiser bought the brand, and it is now produced in Springfield, Missouri.

More Frank's is sold today in the world than any other hot sauce. Cooks say it has more flavor than any other hot sauce, like the other big names Crystal, Trappey's and Texas Pete.

The Original Cincinnati Peanut Butter Brand

In 1906, the Frank Tea & Spice Company got into the peanut butter business with Frank's Jumbo Brand Peanut Butter. Made from a blend of choice no. 1 peanuts, golden toasted, with the bitter hearts and shreds of skin removed, it was old-fashioned style with the oil on top—unhomogenized with the peanut puree. The popularity of the brand caused a new plant at Third and Culvert Streets in Cincinnati to be bought, and then, in 1920, a building at Fifth and Culvert Streets was bought with equipment installed for the cleaning, picking, roasting and grinding of peanuts and packaging of Frank's Jumbo Peanut Butter.

Frank's JUMBO PEANUT BUTTER

Once regarded as only a delicious between meal sandwich spread, peanut butter has, since the Second World War, become recognized as a valuable protein food, rich in B Complex vitamins, calcium and iron. And of all peanut butters, no other has more of the *natural flavor* of fresh salted peanuts than Frank's Jumbo Brand Peanut Butter. Made from a secret blend of choice No. 1 peanuts—golden-toasted; with the bitter hearts and shreds of skin removed but all the natural, golden oil left in—unchanged—Frank's Jumbo Brand Peanut Butter is not only the favorite snack-time spread for millions of youngsters and their parents but the choice of good cooks everywhere who prefer its easy-to-spread, easy-to-blend-in-recipes texture.

Recipes featuring Frank's Jumbo Peanut Butter have added to its wide popularity and use and today its red, white and black label on "double-use jars" is a familiar sight on the shelves of food markets and home pantries.

A 1940s advertisement for Frank's Jumbo Peanut Butter. *Courtesy of John Frank.*

Before the 1940s, peanut butter was just considered a tasty between-meal sandwich spread. But since World War II, it has become known as a valuable protein food, rich in Vitamin B, complex vitamins, iron and calcium.

A representative from Skippy approached the Frank Tea & Spice Company to toll manufacture for it a smooth homogenized peanut butter. But the company declined because it didn't have the equipment necessary to homogenize and wasn't willing to take on the investment needed to purchase that equipment. So, ready-to-spread brands like Skippy and Peter Pan took over the market

The founder of Frank Tea & Spice Company, Jacob Frank. *Courtesy of John Frank.*

with their smooth homogenized peanut butter, which Americans preferred, and Jumbo Brand Peanut Butter became a beloved brand of the past.

OUR LADY OF SPINACH RAVIOLI

There's a brand of ravioli that must be mentioned in Cincinnati that has a more than one-hundred-year-old history: Sacred Heart Church's Spinach Ravioli. The recipe was formulated by the Palazzolo family of Cincinnati for the Sacred Heart Catholic Church Parish of Camp Washington and can only be purchased there. Since 1910, Sacred Heart has been having its annual Ravioli and Spaghetti Dinner twice a year, in April and October. Antonio Palazzolo had a pasta and import company in Cincinnati, and as a member of the Sacred Heart Parish, he supplied his pasta and lent his ravioli recipe to the parish. The signature dish of the event is, of course, the spinach ravioli, made with spinach and ricotta cheese. Each "pocket of joy" is the size of a credit card, and they are bathed in homemade sauce and served piping hot with two meatballs.

Sacred Heart church ladies manually separating the delicious homemade spinach ravioli for their annual church dinner. *Courtesy of Sacred Heart Catholic Church.*

At each dinner, 210,000 ravioli are sold, along with 23,000 meatballs, six hundred gallons of sauce and seven hundred pounds of spaghetti, all made and served by volunteers, some of whom are third- and fourth-generation Palazzolos. The old grade school cafeteria fills up with people from all parts of the city, including local politicians and the foodie famous, some of whom have been coming to the dinner since they were kids.

Mocking the Turtle

When Cincinnatians think of native dishes that have been around for many generations, there's a holy trinity of sorts: Cincinnati chili, goetta and mock turtle soup. Both real turtle soup and mock turtle soup had been popular in Cincinnati among the German immigrants since the mid-nineteenth century. There are many references in the German newspapers showing that turtle soup was served free with a beer at local bars like Peter Hubert's Saloon in Cumminsville. Made with local snapping turtles, Cincinnati's version was less chunky, less tomato-y and also not served with sherry.

It is said that Cincinnati-raised William Howard Taft liked it so much that he brought his own turtle soup chef with him to the White House. At six feet, two inches tall and 315 pounds, Taft still holds the honor of being the heaviest president of the United States. Campbell's soup even tried a canned version in the 1920s that didn't last very long. Mock turtle soup's popularity waned in the 1960s, and it retained popularity in only a few regions—one of those regions being Cincinnati.

As turtle meat became hard to obtain, the mock turtle soup became more prevalent. Original recipes called for meat that mimicked the texture of turtle meat—calf's brains, whole calves' heads and the hooves and tails. Some mock turtle soups even called for a mix of tripe, tendon and sweetbreads, sounding more like the ingredients in a Vietnamese pho than an American soup.

Mock turtle soup was so popular in England that the Mock Turtle became a character in Lewis Carroll's *Alice in Wonderland*. The melancholy character had a turtle shell but also parts of a calf used in the famous soup—head, hooves and tail. In Germany, mock turtle soup was popular in the Oldenburg and Ammerland regions, dating back to the time of the union of the Kingdom of Hanover to the Kingdom of Great Britain, with the coronation in 1714 of Hanoverian-born King George I. Many Cincinnati German immigrants were from these areas and brought this dish with them to Cincinnati.

Cincinnati's own canned brand, Worthmore Mock Turtle Soup, has been around since 1918. Founder Phil Hock was a butcher but gave up the meat when sales of his turtle soup took off. The company now operates on the campus of the old Bruckmann Brewery at the Ludlow viaduct. Its smokestack blazoning Worthmore Soup can be seen deep into the valley.

Cincinnati's version of mock turtle soup is made with lean beef, hardboiled eggs, ketchup, vinegar and a variety of spices. Cincinnati's version didn't call for calves' brains or off cuts of beef. Cincinnati was surrounded by both pork and beef slaughterhouses, so there was no shortage of meat in Greater Cincinnati in the nineteenth century. The soup is very sweet and sour or tangy, sort of like a German version of sweet and sour soup. It's not chunky and has the consistency of Cincinnati chili. It's even served with the same crunchy oyster crackers that are served alongside the chili. Local family restaurants like the Hitching Post and Quatman Café still serve it as a standard dish.

Cincinnati Mock Turtle Soup

2 pounds each ground veal, pork and beef
1 bottle of ketchup
3 tablespoons salt
¼ teaspoon pepper
1 tablespoon allspice
1 cup carrots, chopped
juice of 3 lemons, plus a few slices
red table wine
1 cup dry browned flour
half dozen hardboiled eggs, peeled

In a large pot with the meat, add water to just cover. To water add 1 bottle ketchup, 3 tablespoons salt, ¼ teaspoon pepper, 1 tablespoon allspice, carrots and juice of 3 lemons. Also put in a few slices of lemons. Add 8 ounces of red wine for every 3 gallons of soup. Cook meat until tender, about 3 hours. Brown 1 cup of flour dry in a pan. About half an hour before the soup is done, add brown flour and hardboiled eggs.

Cincinnati Ice Cream Wars

In Cincinnati, there are really only two local ice cream choices—Graeter's and Aglamesis—both of which have been around for more than one hundred years. Each uses a different method of preparation: Graeter's uses the French pot method, and Aglamesis uses a more traditional method. Both have made it through trends that put others out of business. Novelty products like Eskimo Pies and Good Humor bars created an ice cream war on the streets during the 1920s. Sugar and milk rationing during World War II caused issues with product supply and pricing. The growth of Dairy Queen and the trend of soft-serve ice cream in the 1970s led to competitive pressures that both companies responded to successfully. Now they are competing with soft-serve yogurt companies like Yagoot and Orange Leaf, as well as healthier, low-sugar, low-fat options. Local names like French Bauer, Cupid Ice Cream and May Fair Ice Cream are less known and competition from the past, but United Dairy Farmers Homemade Ice Cream and Kroger's Private Selection brands still offer competition on retail shelves. Aglamesis and Graeter's go head to head on their Black Raspberry Chocolate Chip, which is a top seller for both.

The Graeter's story starts in 1868, when Louis Graeter moved to Cincinnati and sold French pot ice cream in a street market in 1870. The French pot method uses a pot that rotates in the center of the machine. The frozen cream is scraped off the sides by hand and incorporated into the still liquid center. This careful process creates a very dense product.

Louis married Regina Berger in 1900, and they sold ice cream out of the front of their house at 967 East McMillen in Walnut Hills. Originally, the Graeters also sold oysters in addition to their ice cream according to early advertisements, most probably to make best use of his ice. After Louis Graeter was struck and killed by a streetcar in 1916, Regina stuck with the old-world method and opened another location in Hyde Park in 1922. During the Depression, Regina's sons, Wilmer and Paul, joined the business, bought out a bankrupt printing plant in Mount Auburn in 1935 and retrofit it into their ice cream plant.

World War II sugar rationing put a crimp on things, but Graeter's was able to stay afloat, offering relief to war-weary Cincinnatians. Wilmer invented the signature chocolate chip flavor series, and the third generation—Dick, Lou, John and Kathy Graeter—stepped into the business.

In 1984, Graeter's opened its first franchised store in Kentucky, and over the next twenty years, it opened more than two dozen more franchised stores. In 1987, Graeter's started selling the ice cream in Kroger's stores, and now it can be seen in more than two thousand stores nationwide.

Today, Bob, Chip and Richard Graeter, the fourth generation, have leadership of the company. In 2010, they led the move to a brand-new production plant in Bond Hill, right off Interstate 75, to service a continually growing market.

Graeter's most popular flavor is Black Raspberry Chocolate Chip, made with mammoth pieces of Peter's chocolate and Oregon black raspberries. Its Classic Flavors include Cookies 'n' Cream, Salted Caramel, Butter Pecan, Cinnamon, Eggnog, Peppermint Stick, Oregon Field Strawberry, Coffee, Dutch Milk Chocolate and Madagascar Vanilla Bean.

Graeter's Signature Chip Flavors are Black Cherry Chocolate Chip, Black Raspberry Chocolate Chip, Toffee Chocolate Chip, Double Chocolate Chip, Mocha Chocolate Chip, Coconut Chocolate Chip, Chocolate Coconut Almond Chocolate Chip, Chocolate Chip, Buckeye Blitz, Peanut Butter Chocolate Chip, Mint Chocolate Chip and Cookie Dough Chocolate Chip.

Today's soda counter at the Oakley Aglamesis store is the original from its opening in 1913. *Courtesy of the Aglamesis family.*

It also brings in seasonal specialties like peach and specials like Elena's BlueBerry Pie for a special cause. To cater to healthier tastes, Graeter's also offers gelato, sorbet and low-glycemic ice cream versions. Whatever your choice, Graeter's is *the* best ice cream to many, including Oprah Winfrey.

THE AGLAMESIS STORY STARTS with two brothers, Thomas and Nicholas, who were born in Sparta, Greece. Thomas left Sparta at age sixteen after his father died, with the responsibility of supporting his large family. He settled in Cincinnati, looking for that opportunity. A year later, his brother Nicholas joined him, and both worked at ice cream shops downtown in the Old Arcade, a series of shops and saloons where Carew Tower stands today, to learn the secrets of the craft.

They saved enough money in 1908 to open their own store, the Metropolitan, in the then booming Norwood neighborhood. They churned all their ice cream by hand, using rock salt as the freezing agent before modern refrigeration. They delivered to the fashionable wealthy class of Norwood, soon developing a reputation of having the fastest horse team in town. Their business grew, and they added candymaking to their ice cream products.

In 1913, the brothers opened their second location in the neighborhood of Oakley. They went all out, importing marble countertops from Portugal (and embellishing the counter with Tiffany lamps), tile floors, sculptured ceilings and a player piano. Even in its time it was considered an exotic place to meet. In 1922, the brothers added a modern ice cream plant to the Oakley location.

The Depression caused the brothers to sell the Metropolitan in Norwood, and their business in Oakley became known as Aglamesis Brothers.

In 1950, when Nicholas passed away and Thomas's health declined, Thomas's son, James T. Aglamesis, took over leadership. Over the years, Aglamesis has gained a national reputation for outstanding quality for its ice cream and candy from the *New York Times*, the *Chicago Tribune*, the History Channel, the Food Network and *Bon Appétit* magazine. With a second location in the Montgomery Square shopping center, their Oakley location is unchanged and remains one of the last intact soda fountains in the Cincinnati area.

Its flavors include Cinnamon, Rum Raisin, Butter Pecan, Banana, Black Raspberry Chocolate Chip, Coffee, Cookies-N-Cream, Chocolate Chip, Dutch Holland Chocolate, Double Chocolate Chip, Mint, French Vanilla, Mocha Chip and Strawberry. It still makes its chocolate-covered cremes and caramels from scratch. It does not use wax or preservatives in its chocolate, so no films develop in your mouth, only the velvety texture of handmade chocolates. For Aglamesis, a third-generation family-owned business, it's always "ice cream and candy made the sincere way."

SCHNECKEN BECKONS

What the hecken *ist* schnecken, you ask? Translated from German as "snails," it's a melt-in-your-mouth, ooey-gooey, buttery sweet roll–like confection shaped like a snail. Technically it's a rich yeast dough filled with sugar, cinnamon, raisins and nuts and then rolled and cut. Three of the cut spirals are stuffed into a buttered loaf pan and baked upside down. When the schnecken are turned out from their pan, the sugar and butter have formed a rich caramel-like glaze over the pastry. It's the great-grandfather to the Cinnabon cinnamon roll. Brought over to Cincinnati by German bakers, one of the most beloved and only surviving examples of this is the Virginia Bakery's schnecken, which used to be on Ludlow Avenue next to the Ludlow Avenue Skyline Chili Parlor. Virginia's schnecken has been called "a heavenly morsel," a "golden brick of pastry," an "outstanding confection" and even "a reason to get up in the morning."

Started in 1927 by Bill Thies, Virginia Bakery was known far and wide for its schnecken, which would come out only around the Christmas holiday. Bill's father, German immigrant Wilhelm Thies, had owned a bakery on the west end of Cincinnati with his wife, Hattie, before being killed in a holdup at the bakery. Bill and brother Carl helped their mom run the bakery until Bill went off on his own and bought Virginia Bakery, named after a previous owner. Bill passed the bakery to his son, Howard, who passed it to his son, Tom. The popularity of schnecken peaked in the 1950s and then in the 1980s. During its later peak, Virginia Bakery would sell as many as ten thousand loaves during a holiday run. The pastry was so popular that Virginia Bakery had an official "schnecken club"—buy a dozen and get one free. For many years, the bakery has shipped thousands of schnecken to homesick Cincinnati expats around the world.

Virginia Bakery made schnecken the old-fashioned way, by hand, since 1927. It's something that can't be made in mixers because the heat will melt the butter, and you won't get the effect of the layers. Tom Thie, the last

Virginia Bakery schnecken is made in three snail-like rolls and is now made seasonally by Busken Bakery. *Courtesy of the Thies family.*

owner of Virginia Bakery, didn't know if the recipe came from Germany with his great-grandfather Wilhelm or if it was created on American soil.

Tom closed the bakery in 2000 and made schnecken for a limited time during the holidays until a fall from a tree in 2005 made him stop for good. He then licensed the secret schnecken recipe to Busken Bakery, which also brings it out, under the Virginia Bakery name, during the holidays. Some say that the Busken version is not as sticky and buttery as the original Virginia recipe they remember.

Get Stung with the Beehive Cake

Little Dutch Bakery was founded in 1929 by Franklin Girmann, and he moved it in 1954 to its current location on Hamilton Avenue in the Mount Healthy area. It is now owned and run by Frank's grandson, Chris Girmann, and his wife, Mary. Although they have great doughnuts, tea cookies, cakes and pies, they are best known for their award-winning Beehive Coffee Cake, voted "Best in the City" by *Cincinnati* magazine.

This famous coffeecake has been brought over from Germany and handed down through three generations of the Girmann family. It's a melt-in-your-mouth pastry flavored with honey and is similar to Cincinnati schnecken except that it's lighter and less rich.

To make the coffeecake, Chris sprinkles dough with cinnamon and sugar, rolls it into a log shape and then cuts the dough crosswise into chunks. The dough goes into honey- and brown sugar–glazed pans and gets another dose of honey and brown sugar, along with a sprinkle of pecans.

The beehive comes in two sizes and is either iced with caramel icing, the most popular choice, or white-iced. Chris will even ice it in chocolate if asked. To serve, it is recommended to be lightly heated in the oven and accompanied with a glass of milk.

The Polish Pre-Lenten Calorie Bomb

Bonomini Bakery in Northside is the best place in Greater Cincinnati to find the Polish paczki doughnut, as voters proved in *Cincinnati* magazine's Best of Cincinnati many years running. Although they look like the German

Berliner, an American Bismark or jelly doughnut, paczki are made from an especially egg-rich dough, deep fried and stuffed with a variety of fruit and crème fillings. They help to fill the pastry void between the end of Christmas and the beginning of Lent, as they're only available from late January to mid-February, when Ash Wednesday puts an end to sweet indulgences.

The Busken Bakery Empire

Busken Bakery was founded in 1928 by Joe Busken Sr. with help from his wife, Daisey. With no particular grand vision of the empire that his bakery would become, he made it through the Depression with a reputation for good quality products and extremely sliceable breads. They now have ten chain stores across the city. With a variety of great products and a commissary in Hyde Park that's open twenty-four hours, their most famous product is their yellow iced smiley-faced cookies. It's a cakey sugar cookie with a touch of almond flavor. Like the Oreo cookie, people have all different ways to eat a Busken smiley-faced cookie. Some lick the face off before eating, some eat the icing off, some dip in milk and some dip in coffee or tea.

Pumpkin Pie Wars

Busken Bakery and Frisch's restaurants have always had a friendly rivalry as to whose pumpkin pie is the most popular or best in Cincinnati. In the fall of 2010, Frisch's launched a new billboard campaign for its pumpkin pies in anticipation of the holiday season. A billboard with the slogan "Hello Pumpkin" was "inadvertently" located over the Busken's flagship store in Hyde Park. Busken quickly launched its own retort, quickly buying an adjacent billboard that read, "That's Mr. Pumpkin to you, Big Boy." Into 2011, the chains traded digs on billboards like boxers circling each other in a ring. Frisch's then put up another billboard over the Busken flagship store with the picture of a simple pumpkin pie, saying, "You had me at hello." Busken retorted again with the adjacent billboard: "Sorry Big Boy, this pumpkin's taken." The Busken brothers even put a Busken apron on the fiberglass Big Boy statue outside its Mainliner Restaurant and encased the

An ad for Frisch's pumpkin pie shows the delicacy that sells ninety thousand pies during a sixteen-week holiday period. *Courtesy of Frisch's.*

Big Boy sandwich he carries with a Busken pie box, filming the entire thing and posting on their website.

Both companies clearly benefitted from the battle. Frisch's, which typically sells 90,000 pumpkin pies during its sixteen-week holiday selling window, saw an uptick of 5 percent, while Busken, which typically sells 2,500 pumpkin pies, saw a 20 percent jump in sales.

THE MANISCHEWITZ MATZO EMPIRE

The matzo cracker might seem simple to the naked eye, but the laws of kosher preparation have made it complicated. Matzo dough must not rise, so the entire process must be completed in under eighteen minutes. In pre–Civil War America, eighteen minutes from mix to bake was considered fast food. Before the mid-nineteenth century, matzo was baked in synagogues with ovens specifically designed for that purpose. But after the mid-nineteenth century, small bakeries started making matzo. Matzo-making machines were designed to make the process more efficient. But to many Jews, the new processes were not in line with kosher law. So, to the faithful, matzo was a luxury only the wealthy could afford.

That changed about a century ago when Rabbi Dov Behr Manischewitz started baking matzo in Cincinnati in 1889. Behr Manischewitz came to Cincinnati in 1885 with his wife, Nesha, and three small children to serve

Dov Manischewitz, the man who made matzo square and built a kosher empire. *Courtesy of the Hebrew Union College.*

as a kosher butcher for a group of Orthodox Jews from his hometown in Lithuania. Behr saw an opportunity in making matzo available to all Jews, regardless of wealth. He designed and patented a machine that cut and baked matzo in uniform squares and packaged in shippable boxes. This made matzo available for the common Jew.

By 1889, ads for Manischewitz matzo were appearing in the *American Israelite*, offering the "kosherest of matzos, matzo meal." Three years later, he announced in an ad "new matzos machines whereby this year's matzos will be most beautiful to behold and most palatable to the taste." In ten years, Behr bought his competitor, Bing Bakery, around the corner from his West Sixth Street baker.

Behr's 1911 patent for a conveyor belt sandwiched between upper and lower heating elements indicates his spirit of creativity and innovation, despite his conservative Orthodoxy. This allowed Manischewitz to produce more, better and cheaper matzo than ever before. The square crackers were considered top quality and marketed as a luxury item, coming in a wooden box. It also saved on waste. The corners cut off round matzos could not be reused because they might have time to rise, which was against the kosher recipe.

Being able to ship around the country and internationally helped him grow the business. In 1913, he opened a second bakery on West Eighth Street in Lower Price Hill and added capacity to the existing bakery on West Sixth Street. In 1914, Behr died, and the business passed to his five sons, with Jake at the helm.

As the company grew, East Coast customers dominated the demand, and they opened a bakery in New Jersey in 1932, moving headquarters there in the 1950s. In 1947, Max Manischewitz developed an agreement with Monarch Wine to produce a kosher wine. In 1954, another plant was purchased in Vineland, New Jersey, for production of chicken soup, borscht and gefilte fish. The first non-Passover product, Tam Tam crackers, was added to the lineup as kosher food became synonymous with "fresh."

One by one, the Manischewitz family moved to the New York area, except Howard, who oversaw the Lower Price Hill factory until its closing in 1958. The family sold the company in 1990 to Kohlberg & Company for $42.5 million, at the time controlling 80 percent of the world matzo market.

Shur Good

Mama's Cookies are a brand that many baby boomers remember from their childhood. The round crunchy cookies with sugar on top came in several flavors: regular sugar cookies, chocolate, almond, lemon and macaroon. They were made so popular locally because they advertised on the *Uncle Al Show* from 1954 until 1984 and were distributed by local Shur Good Biscuit Company, founded in 1926. Uncle Al's patronage sold so many Mama's Cookies he was nicknamed "King of the Rings." He and the kids would sing a variation of the "Shortening Bread" song for their jingle on the show.

The hole in the center of the cookies was just big enough that a kid could fit his finger through a number of them and eat them down off his finger.

After a hiatus of thirteen years, investors bought the manufacturer and reintroduced Mama's Cookies in 1997, again using local Cincinnati Shur Good Biscuit Company as its main distributor and capitalizing on baby boomer nostalgia.

Barq's Red Pop

Although Barq's parent company was founded in Biloxi, Mississippi, in 1898, one of its most loved products, red pop, was invented in Cincinnati.

The French chew is a popular local candy invented by the Doscher Company, founded in 1861 by German immigrant Claus Doscher. *Author's collection.*

Contract bottlers all around the country would buy root beer and crème soda concentrates from Biloxi and mix and bottle them in their local plants.

Richard Tuttle, Hugh Carmichael and Albert Badanes founded the Barq Bottling Company in Cincinnati in 1937. Tuttle started adding red dye to the amber crème soda, creating the red pop now known as Barq's Red Crème Soda, which would become a kid favorite.

Soon after, the parent company began adding the red dye to its concentrate. Tuttle went on with his chemist to create other flavors—grape, lemon-lime and orange sodas. Sales took off with these new flavors, and the three men realized success as the franchise that covered Greater Cincinnati established plants in Hamilton and Portsmouth, Ohio. Tuttle bought out his two partners in the 1960s and was president of the Cincinnati Bottling Company until he retired in 1980.

SELECTED BIBLIOGRAPHY

BOOKS

Alpern, Laura. *Manishewitz, the Matzo Family: The Making of an American Jewish Icon.* Brooklyn, NY: KTAV Publishing House Inc., 2008.

Beischel, Cynthia, and Tom Thie. *Virginia Bakery Remembered.* Charleston, SC: The History Press, 2012.

Fischer, Linda. *The Whiskey Merchant's Diary: An Urban Life in the Emerging Midwest.* Athens: Ohio University Press, 2007.

Gearhart, John. *Frankly Speaking: Fifty Years of Progress, 1896–1946.* Cincinnati, OH: Frank Tea & Spice Company, 1946.

Glier, Dan. *Glier's Goetta Recipe Book: A Guide to Glier's Goetta.* Covington, KY: Glier's Meats Inc., 2006.

Turizziana, Robert. *Cincinnati Fine Restaurants.* Cincinnati, OH: Restaurants International, 1989.

Selected Bibliography

Interviews

Buscani, Pete, of LaRosa's Pizza. Interview with the author, January 2015.

Frank, John, of Frank Tea & Spice Company. Interview with the author, December 2014.

Graeter, Richard, of Graeter's Ice Cream; Charlie Howard, of Gold Star Chili; Evan Andrews, of Montgomery Inn; Pete Buscani, of LaRosa's; and Karen Maier, of Frisch's. AMA Signature Speaker Series, March 27, 2015.

Gramaglia, Pat, of Pasquale's Pizza. Interview with the author, January 2015.

Kahn, Bill, of Chili Bowl. Interview with the author, January 2015.

Miscellaneous City Sources

Cincinnati city directories, 1919–84. Public Library of Cincinnati and Hamilton County, Cincinnati, Ohio.

Western Hills High School yearbooks, 1946–66. Price Hill Historical Society, Cincinnati, Ohio.

INDEX

W

Z

ABOUT THE AUTHOR

Dann Woellert is a marketing manager and has been in the product marketing field for more than a decade. He writes the food blog "Dann Woellert the Food Etymologist," which discusses the origin of local and national delicacies. Dann is affiliated with the Cincinnati Preservation Association, the Cincinnati Historical Society and the German American Citizen's league and has created and led historic tours for Architreks. He has received the Ohioiana Award for Literary and Artistic Achievement three times.